Strewing the Pateran:

The Gypsies of

Thorney Hill

John Pateman

Pateran Press
11 Windsor Close
Sleaford, NG34 7NL

First Edition, 2008

ISBN 978-0-956081-6-1

All rights reserved. No part of this publication may be reproduced, stored in a retrieval system, or transmitted in any form or by any means – electronic, mechanical, photo copying, recording or otherwise, without the prior permission of the copyright owner.

All extracts from other published works are acknowledged and permission has been sought to have them reproduced in this book.

Acknowledgements

Julia Berlin
The Revd. Canon P.C.Elkins
Tim Goddard
Hampshire Record Office
Janet Keet-Black
Robert Dawson
Lesley Doe
Stephen Doe
Sharon Floate
Eddie Higgins
Ruth Lavender
Alan McGowan
Annette Pateman
Dave & Susie Pateman
M.W.Penfold
Mrs Strang
Patricia White

Dedication

To Amelia Goddard, whose paintings gave me the title and chapter headings for this book. The descriptions of her paintings at the start of each chapter are taken from *The House of the Open Door* (Gillington, 1908).

Contents

1. In Holly Shelter

2. Gypsies Halting by The Ling

3. Lighting-Up

4. Mary Stanley

5. Strewing the Pateran

6. Chronology

7. Families

8. Sources

1. In Holly Shelter

"Once more the scene shifts, and one finds oneself in the "Holly Shelter" on Thorney Hill, amongst a motley throng of men, women and children; there is warmth and colour everywhere; autumn glow, fire-glow, and glow of Gypsy faces. The smoke of burning furze-fuel floats through the green forest spaces; you hear the chavis' saviben and roviben, the chais' rapid rokerin' and the gilyin' of the chablos, as they raise their peculiar sing-song nasal chant, in strict time, as if to a fiddle and tambourine accompaniment, the old Forest ballads, passed orally down from one generation to another: the forest murder legend of the "Brake o' Briars", the forest love tale of "The Green Bushes", and the oft told tale of "The Three Gypsies" :

"There was three Gypsies all in a row,
And they sang brisk and bonny, O!
They sang so high and they sang so low
Till downstairs came the lady, O!

They gave to she a nut-a-meg brown,
And a cake of the very best ginger, O!
But she gave to they a far better thing,
For she gave them the ring from her finger, O!

Now there was three Gypsies all of a row,
And they was hanged all just so;
For they was hanged all of a row
For stealing the yellow castle's lady, O!"

This ballad was "sung at Thorney Hill, Hants, in July 1908, by Thomas Pateman, a middle-aged Gypsy." (Gillington, 1908). I came across the Patemans of Thorney Hill while carrying out research in the *Journal of the Gypsy Lore Society* (JGLS) at Kensington Central Library. An article entitled *Affairs of Egypt* (Crofton, 1907) described Thorney Hill as the "New Forest alleged Gypsy village" :

"On 3 June 1907 the *Morning Leader* (see also *Christchurch Times*, 15 June 1907, and *Northern Echo*, Darlington, 10 July 1907) had an article on this subject with photographic views of Thorny Hill church, "a Gypsy flower-seller" and "a typical Gypsy cottage". Thorny Hill is near Bransgore, on the outskirts of the New Forest, and "for many years past" the population has been principally Gypsies, "now about 100" [not 700, as stated in *JGLS*, New Series, i. 331]. Marriages between them and the rustics are not uncommon. Caravans are seldom seen. The Gypsies live in thatched cottages. In springtime a family or two "get on the move", and return when summer is over. All have adopted English names, Scott and Pateman being the favourites. They are very clannish, and quite commonly three generations live together in the same cottage. The elder women cling to the Romany headdress; ear rings are *de rigueur* for both sexes. The women go to Bournemouth on Tuesdays, Thursdays, and Saturdays to sell flowers [the wild ox-eye daisy was a great favourite of them ten years ago]. The men drive them in pony carts to Christchurch, eight miles distant, and thence they go by train to Bournemouth: the double journey costs sixpence, and they often invest £2 in flowers. They keep cows and "requisition" the Forest ponies.

On June 12, in the *Morning Leader*, W.G.Reed, a resident near Thorney Hill, challenged the foregoing account, stating that "just three men wear earrings; strawberry-growing, brick making, and farming are the chief industries; there are only three families of Scotts and three of Patemans, but there are ten distinct families of Broomfields, who are positively not of Gypsy origin." On June 7 the *Hampshire Post* reported that Robert Pateman and his brother Sydney, Gypsies, encamped at Sarisbury near Southampton, were fined for "using bad language on the highway."

Thorney Hill

In July 2003 I went on a camping holiday to the New Forest and stayed at Holmsley Camp Site, which is very near Thorney Hill. One evening I took a drive out to Thorney Hill, which is halfway between Bransgore and Burley, and between the New Forest and the Avon Valley. I saw a cross on the Ordnance Survey map which denoted a "place of worship", but as I drove up and down the Burley Road I could not see a building which resembled a church. Instead I saw what looked like a stately home and so I parked the car and got out to take a look. As I approached the gate to this property I saw a sign which announced the building as All Saints Church, Thorney Hill.

I walked up to the church, which was locked, and wandered around the church yard. I saw many gravestones with the name Pateman on them, and I started to take notes. I noticed a freshly dug grave with many flowers on it in the name of a Mr Cooper. As I was looking at this grave a man and woman arrived to place more flowers on the grave. I started talking to them and found out that they were the brother and sister of the buried man. I contacted one of the churchwardens and arranged to visit All Saints the next day. It was a glorious summer day with a blue sky and the Forest was in full leaf. I was given a guided tour of the church and put in touch with Canon Patrick Elkins, who sent me these notes by Brigadier Arthur Fortescue, a relation of Lord Manners:

"This beautiful church was built to the glory of God and in memory of the Hon. Mary Christine Manners, eldest child of Lord John and Lady Constance Manners. The Manners family lived about a mile away at Avon Tyrrell. Mary Christine, whose image can be seen over the main door, died aged 17 in 1904. Her grieving parents commissioned the young architect Detmar Blow to design and build this place of worship to commemorate her life and serve the people of Thorney Hill. It was dedicated in 1906 and remains in regular use each Sunday as the centre of Church of England worship in Thorney Hill in the parish of St Mary, Bransgore.

The remarkable design reflects what Blow had seen and learned in Venice while studying with John Ruskin. An unusual feature is the church's North-South orientation instead of the customary East-West position. Its imposing structure dominates the landscape and can be seen for miles away across the valley. The building reflects the contemporary Art Nouveau fashion and the age of the Arts and Crafts Movement. The only additional art work in 1906 was the commemorative panel under the balcony recording Mary Christine's death. The design and lettering is by the young Eric Gill, just setting out on his career as a sculptor of great genius. Art historians believe it is his finest work in this genre.

The Manner's story at Thorney Hill begins when John, third Baron Manners married Constance Hamlyn Fane in 1885. Lord John and Lady Constance were better known to friends as 'Hoppy' (he had a springy style of walking) and 'Con'. The Hamlyn Fane family of Clovelly in Devon also owned land in the New Forest. In fact Constance was born at Avon Tyrrell Cottage in 1852. The cottage was replaced by Avon Tyrrell House (another Manners commission) completed in the early 1890s by the great architect, William Lethaby. This was now to be the home of the newly weds and their growing family – Mary Christine, twins Betty and Angela, John and Francis.

In 1882 Lord Manners had won the Grand National on his horse 'Seaman'. A wager had been set up for him to choose, train and ride a horse to win this famous race. Legend has it that his success (and the proceeds of the wager) enabled him to build this wonderful house for his bride. The church also followed as an expression of love for their first born, so quickly taken from them.

Another tragedy was to overtake the family ten years later. On 1 September 1914, barely four weeks into the Great War, John (the heir) was killed in the Retreat from Mons at the age of 22. Lady Cynthia Asquith wrote in her diary that 'Avon was the frame for John' and with his death there was nothing left except those things that merely emphasised his loss. As the war progressed it would be a multiplying grief leaving few families untouched. John's memory lives on in the marvellous bronze by the great Australian sculptor who had made his home in Britain Sir Bertram MacKennal – a pupil of that great French master, Rodin. The cenotaph on which the effigy rests is by Eric Gill, as is also the epitaph and the mourning angels.

In 1920 Lady Con also died at 58. Lord Manners commissioned one last great work to honour her memory – the magnificent 'Te Deum' mural from the floor to the apse of the sanctuary by Phoebe Traquair. It was Traquair's last masterpiece in this art of mural painting. In 1920 she was the first woman to be admitted as an honorary member of the Royal Scottish Academy. She completed the mural in 1922 at the age of 70. In her letters she tells of the hard physical struggle climbing the scaffolding to do the painting. This homely and restrained memorial was a fitting conclusion to Phoebe's long life in the service of art. It was appropriate also that Lady Con who had consistently patronised the arts should herself be commemorated by such an expression of beauty and Christian hope. The figures in the mural are of the Manners family, friends and famous people. We find real people dressed in costume representing Biblical characters, or just themselves. Baby Jesus is Con's youngest child – Francis. All the family are there together with Raymond Asquith (the Prime Minister's son, killed 1916 and specially befriended by Con), Lord William Cecil (Bishop of Essex), Lord Tennyson (Poet Laureate), William Blake (Traquair's inspiration and muse) and the two famous physicians Louis Pasteur and Lord Lister. The mural is also a war memorial for the many soldiers who had been killed in the service of their country – and for a small community such as Thorney Hill the casualties were very high, affecting many families."

There is also a War Memorial in the churchyard. Among the names on this War Memorial are H. Pateman and W. Pateman, who both died in the Great War. There is also W. Pateman who died in the Second World War. The W. Pateman killed in the Great War was Walter Pateman of the Hampshire Regiment, who was killed in action on 1 September 1916. My great uncle was also a Walter Pateman, and he was killed in action on 27 February 1917 - see *Seven Steps to Glory – Private Pateman goes to war* (Romany and Traveller Family History Society, 2002).

Gypsies still live in the Council houses opposite the church. They settled at Thorney Hill originally to tend the brick kilns at night. Until the 1960s they were living in The Hollies, at the Cross Ways, next to Magpie Green. They had bender tents spread over holly bushes and asbestos sheds which belonged to the World War Two American airbase. The concrete foundations can still be seen in dry weather. The Gypsy community regards All Saints as "their" church. The New Forest Patemans can be traced back to the 1830's when John Pateman first moved into the area, having travelled down from Bisham in Buckinghamshire. I am now trying to establish a link between this branch of the family, and my Pateman's, who were mostly born in Kent:

Paultons: "Gypsy families roamed the roads in small family groups. They did not generally travel great distances, for instance, the New Forest Gypsies would not generally travel much further than Southampton or Salisbury. One time that Gypsies did travel further was hop picking time, and the New Forest gypsies often travelled to Kent, because strawberry picking and the local harvest were over, and there was no hoeing to be done at that time of year".

Artists and Writers
Many artists and writers were attracted to the New Forest to write about and paint its natural beauty, its flora and fauna, and its Gypsies. The paintings of Gypsy life by Amelia Goddard, who lived near Thorney Hill, inspired the title and chapter headings of this book. The great artist, Augustus John, became a close friend and patron of the Gypsies. But it was another artist, Sven Berlin, who really got to know them well. The story of his life with the Gypsies at Shave Green is told in *Dromengro*. This remarkable book, which was first published in 1971, was reissued in 2003 by Finishing Publications Ltd, PO Box 70, 105 Whitney Drive, Stevenage, Hertfordshire, SG1 4DF, www.svenberlin.com.

Finishing Publications are engaged in a long term project aimed at making Sven Berlin's works more accessible to the public. This will include a wonderful series of drawings he made, known as the "Shave Green" drawings, which mainly depict the people of the Forest. Also available is *Virgo in Exile* (1996), which opens with Sven's departure from St Ives, in a horse and cart and describes his life on the Isle of Wight and then the New Forest, where he even had a private zoo. *The Other Man* (2005) is the last part of Sven's autobiographical memoirs or "autosvenography".

I am very grateful to Finishing Publications and to Sven's widow, Mrs Julia Berlin, for allowing me to quote extracts from *Dromengro* in this book. In my correspondence with Mrs Berlin, she also told me more about life with Sven and the Gypsies at Shave Green:

"Sven started out as a painter and was always a painter. The eras of paintings follow groups of years: Pre War St Ives 1936-39; Post War 1945-53; Forest paintings including Forest and Gypsy paintings 1953-70; we left the Forest and went to the Isle of Wight 1970-75. The Dorset Collection covers 1970 until when my Sven died in 1999. Stone cutting and bronze casting were also performed. He had his own foundry at home farm and cast his own bronze."

"My husband Sven made it very clear that he did not live in Shave Green but visited. As he put it, 'they had nothing, I had nothing but whatever was amongst us was shared.' He always had campsites in the Forest until he was moved on."

"On the long road out of Lyndhurst to Minstead was the New Forest foxhounds. My dad Harry Lenthall was a huntsman. About half a mile further along that road was Shave Green. Benny Wells, Harriet Wells and Rosie Miller used the bus stop on that road, and I would see them all there at seven o' clock in the morning. They had their great baskets of flowers which they were taking for sale in Southampton. They loved going up stairs and riding in the front seats, they became so excited, I remember."

"Benny Wells when he was dying of throat cancer used to call on us at home farm, we were newly married, it was about 1963. I was a young girl of 19. He came for the warmth and to watch the TV, his favourite was 'Take Your Pick'. One evening when he left he held out his hand to me and three beautiful Georgian half crowns fell into my hand. Two I had made into brooches for my mum and Sven and a silver coin ring. I still have them with that vivid memory. My regret was that I couldn't take Benny's whippet as he wanted me to home it after his death. I love whippets and used to breed them but for some reason at that point I was unable to take him, probably because I had a large greyhound and six other dogs at the time."

"I well remember that when Sven and I drove back to the Forest from Dorset, a figure gleening through the gorse on the old site of Thorney Hill looked up and Sven remarked 'That's Black Fred having a last search around'. It's an image that has remained in my mind ever since."

The Gypsies
There are many accounts of Gypsy life in the New Forest over the years. Here are some snapshots from 1891, 1895, 1899 and 1912:

Louisa Stokes: "I was born in the New Forest, a Gypsy, on June 3rd 1891, one of a family of eleven. We ate and slept in or around the caravan that we Gypsies always called a 'wagon'. My father never worked so my mother had to go out daily to get a living, pedalling chairs and fancy tables. Usually my older sisters and brothers would go out with mother to help her sell her wares. We smaller ones would stay in a secluded lane or on some common all day to wait for mother's return, sometimes without food until she came home. We seldom had good shoes to wear and often went barefoot for days, until we had a visit from grannie, my father's mother. She was a queenly old lady and loved her only child dearly."

When Louisa was twelve she "begged ten shillings for opening a gate for riders to go through in the New Forest". Her sisters included Rosie, Charlotte, Patience and Priscilla. Among the places which Louisa mentions are Bishops Waltham, Odiham, Southampton, Bournemouth, Basingstoke, Alton, Millbrook, Swaythling, Eastleigh, Hook, Lyndhurst, Brockenhurst, Cadnam, Winchester, Swanick, Four Marks and Andover.

The family travelled a regular route. In the spring Louisa would "pick wild flowers and bunch them up and sell them to the houses". In the summer she would pick strawberries, followed by hops in the autumn: "Since fruit picking had finished, we had been moving around the New Forest and were now making our way towards Alton to start hop picking again." This was her favourite time of year: "Each year we went hop picking and this was the grandest time of all, when we saw a lot of Gypsies all together, some of whom we only saw at hopping time each year."

In the winter they would return to Southampton "to sell wood and mats and chairs, and father buys some holly to sell at Christmas". Louisa describes how "I went to get my swag ready to go out selling…all that day walking in and out of gates hawking the houses". With the return of spring the family would go back on the road and this cycle of seasonal employment and travel would start again.

On their journeys around the Forest they would stay in green lanes. "Most of the house dwellers knew us and never grumbled when we went to their houses for water or when I wanted a letter written." One Christmas they had "a nice tea with a Christmas pudding which we had been given by one of the ladies in a nearby cottage." When Andrew (her future husband) came to visit, Louisa arranged for him to stay with a local woman. "I knew her very well as she had written letters for me many times".

John Wise (1895): "Many people have a vague notion that the Gypsies constitute the most important element of the population of the New Forest, whereas, of course, they are mere cyphers. An amusing enough French author, in a work upon England, has devoted a special chapter to the New Forest, and there paid more attention to the Gypsies than to any one else, and entirely forgets the West Saxon, whose impress is indelibly marked , not only in the language, but in the names of every town, village, and field.

As, however, every one takes a romantic interest in these nomads, we must not entirely pass over them. Here and there still linger a few in whose veins run Indian blood, against whom Henry VIII made bad laws, and Skelton worse rhymes. The principal tribes round Lyundhurst are the Stanleys, the Lees, and Burtons; and near Fordingbridge, the Snells. They live chiefly in the various droves and rides of the Forest, driven from place to place by the policeman, for to this complexion have things come. One of their favourite halting places is amongst the low woods near Wooton, where a dozen or more brown tents are always fluttering in the wind, and as the night comes on the camp fires redden the dark fir stems.

The kingly title formerly held by the Stanleys is now in the possession of the Lees. They all still, to a certain extent, keep up their old dignity, and must by no means be confounded with the strolling outcasts and itinerant beggars who also dwell in the Forest. Their marriages, too, are still observed with strictness, and any man or woman who marries out of the caste, as recently in the case of one of the Lees, who wedded a blacksmith, is instantly disowned. The proverb, too, of honour among thieves is also still kept, and formal meetings are every now and then convened to expel any member who is guilty of cheating his kinsman.

Since the deer have been destroyed in the Forest, life is not to them what it was. They are now content to live upon a stray fowl, or hedgehog, or squirrel, baked whole in a coat of clay, and to gain a livelihood by weaving the heather into mats, and brooms, and beehives. They are, however, mere wanderers and have nothing to do with the soil."

Rose C. De Crespigny and Horace Hutchinson (1899): "The Gypsies of the New Forest are a fairly numerous body, living in vans or tents and paying no taxes – in summer, pitching their camp in the shade of trees, in winter under the sheltering screen of furze and scrub. Fifty years ago the romance with which our fancy surrounds them was something of a reality. Among them there were excellent musicians, some of whom played the violin really well, while the rest would dance to its strains on the greensward according to all the best traditions. Now the violin is scarcely to be heard. Recently a melodeon was among the cherished household goods of a roving family, but in course of years it had grown feeble and asthmatic, and in solemn conclave it was determined that its hour of death had come. Its funeral, with the rites of cremation, was celebrated with some ceremony.

The vans in which the modern Gypsy is wont to travel are often picturesque enough, making bright spots of colour as they journey amongst the Forest trees. A glance into the interior, as they pass, will show neat muslin curtains and even a picture or two by way of ornament. The women of the tribe, more especially, occasionally show an Oriental taste for vivid colouring in the way of red and yellow handkerchiefs, but the majority of the people and their children are clad in the unlovely and ragged garments of the common tramp.

The number of Gypsies in the Forest varies with the seasons and with circumstances. Such an attraction as a fair will draw in many from without the Forest's border, and a fair in prospect will detain many who would otherwise be wandering elsewhere. Their means of livelihood are most precarious, and in winter and times of evil weather their lot must be a very hard one. They earn small sums by the manufacture of clothes' pegs and meat skewers. For the latter there is quite a large demand by butchers about Christmas time. They ply a small trade in rags and rabbit skins, and show much ingenuity in the plaiting of grass mats. In summer they gather nosegays of wild flowers and sell them in the neighbouring towns. In winter, when flowers are lacking, they take the white pith out of rushes, and with a little moss contrive an ingenious and tolerable imitation of moss roses.

There is something peculiarly fitting and engaging in the use that these children of Nature make of the simple things that Nature strews in their way; but the livelihood they derive therefrom, if honest, must, of necessity, be meagre. Some ply the less picturesque, but perhaps more reliable, trade of the tinsmith. In the spring before the bees begin to swarm, they busy themselves with making beehives, which find a ready sale. In the summer many of them move farther up the county, or even so far as the neighbourhood of London, seeking jobs in haymaking, fruit picking, harvesting and hopping. A certain number of them go away for the hopping month only, remaining in the Forest all the rest of the year. They travel, like the planets, in something approaching a circuitous route. In winter a number of them congregate, with their vans, in a field near Fordingbridge, which has been purchased by the tribe as a secure haven during the cold weather. Others dwell in little round topped tents which look hardly tall enough for a man to stand upright in them. To stand upright, however, is no great need of the Gypsy. The recumbent position, as a rule, is good enough for him.

Their tents they move from place to place – on donkey back for preference, by hand cart failing the donkey, and on their own backs as a last resource. The life of the Gypsy is a perpetual repetition of 'move on!' By law they are not allowed to camp for more than twenty four hours in any one spot – nor within a certain radius of it – in one county. It does not trouble the child of Nature to evade this law of a senile civilisation. On the Salisbury side of the Forest runs a road bordered by a generous strip of greensward, furze and general brushwood on either side. It is the boundary road of two counties – Hampshire and Wiltshire. The one broad strip is in one county, the other strip in the other. It is a bore, no doubt, but scarcely a grievous fatigue, for the Egyptian to harness his horse or donkey to his caravan and conduct his household goods across the road, from one county to the other, and so evade the simple law. Their encampments stand on one side or other of the road so long as it pleases them – a picturesque and eloquent endorsement of Mr Bumble's opinion of the law."

Elizabeth Godfrey (1912): "The special forest industries are disappearing; the last charcoal burner's hut is really only preserved as a curiosity. You rarely see the Gypsies platting mats or baskets, though there is an old man who still goes round, and sits by the roadside, reseating your old chairs with cane or rushes.

One of the favourite camping grounds of the Gypsies is a crest of moor, fringed with Scotch firs, called Coldharbour, a name accounted for by some as *Col d'arbres*, 'the ridge or neck of trees'. It may well be, for the pines are a striking feature, very old and in their grouping very lovely, shorn by the prevailing winds into harmonious curves, bending away from the sea; for over Setley Plain the sea winds sweep, and often the sea mists too. Lifting my eyes from my writing, I can see as many as three caravans drawn up in the shade, for it is fair time, and the spot, just aside from the high road, affords a night's shelter to these nomads who travel from fair to fair, pasture too for their horses, and water from a pond formed at the bottom of an old gravel pit just below.

It is generally the vanners who come to this spot, vagrants rather than true Gypsies ('Diddyki', the Romany calls them), and untidy in their leavings, which the genuine Gypsy seldom is. These prefer to set up their snug little tents in the thicket of the Brake just across the plain. Here I have found a young mother with an infant of days in a tent on hoops, not much larger than a gig umbrella, a fire hard by in a bell tent with a hole at the top. Going to pay a call with a pink flannel to wrap the baby in, I found mother and child warm, happy, and content, the former rejoicing in the permission accorded, under these circumstances, of a stay of two weeks. Once I ventured to condole with a Gypsy woman on wild wintry weather in such a tent. She tossed back her jet black hair plaits: 'Oh, I likes it, my dear; I'm used to it, ye see'.

If by nothing else, the Gypsy may be distinguished from the ordinary tramp by his cheerful insouciant outlook on life, as well as a sense of humour not yet quenched by the Missioner, the Board School, and the perpetual harass of having to move on. These three factors, especially the second, tend to stamp out the Gypsy as a race apart, or to make of him a very unsatisfactory low class vagrant – a poor exchange. Unhappily the Missioner is rarely content to bring religion to the Gypsy and leave him a Gypsy still. He must needs try and induce him to abandon his way of life, to forsake his wholesome tent for an insanitary slum, and to send his children to school. If the Board School system is turning out a failure for our little peasants, what can we say for it when it claims the Gypsy? The Gypsy child simply cannot assimilate book learning. He goes in sharp as a needle, cunning as a fox, sagacious with ancient woodland lore, long sighted, keen of ear and scent; he comes out stupid, blear eyed, often slightly deaf. The new knowledge drops away from him in a month; the old has been stamped out. You have made of him a lazy good for nothing, liable to colds and ailments hitherto unknown.

One rainy winter day I met a Gypsy friend of mine and stopped to buy a brush. A little girl of eleven was helping to carry the basket; the wet and mud were squishing out of the poor child's boots, from the burst sides of which a sopped rag of stocking was exuding. I suggested that bare feet would be safer. 'True it is, my lady, and full well I know it, but what can I do? 'Tis the schoolalities, you see; to school she must go, and I don't like for folks to pass remarks on my children.'"

New Forest Voices

It is clear from Louisa Stokes's account that the Gypsies co-existed happily with local communities. The same point was made by Eddy and Cath, "Commoners and farm produce sellers", who were interviewed by Mike Turner in his book *New Forest Voices* (1999). Mike asked them "How did you get on with the Gypsies?":

"Very well. Never ought to have moved them. I've been in their tents. I've tried peg making but I could never get on with it. We used to have a lot of poultry at that time, running loose. They would go into the Forest and lay their eggs. The Gypsies would go and pick a few of them up, but then who could blame them for that? We always found, if we wanted any help, go to the Gypsies. If we'd lost a cow – mind, we'd give them a little if they found the cow - if we'd lost a cow, either got in a bog or anything, the whole encampment nearly'd go out and look for it. Of course, if you cross them in any way, that was different. They didn't forget things like that. I say it was a mistake even to put them into compounds, that was the beginning of the end of them, the break up."

Mike Turner also interviewed Tom, a Gypsy, who was living in a council house in a village just outside the Forest boundary. "I was born at Dibden Purlieu, a little place called Dibden Bottom, in a bender tent. Was Gypsies; I am a Gypsy. People used to come along there and say, that's dirty old Gypsies and things like that; well, we didn't take much notice of them.

A bender tent is some rods bent over and a cloth or something over the top of it. Make it round. More or less like the Saxons used to have, right back in history. We used to use rods – well, hazel sticks really it was, about an inch thick and about seven to eight foot long. All as we had in there was a box, like an orange crate, to have our food off. No chairs or nothing. All we used to turn up…was a black bucket what my mother used to do her washing in, or sit on a box or make yourself up an old bit of a stool. Many a time I've got a bit of straw, a bit of bracken, fern, and made it up in a little heap, put a bit of cloth on it and sit on that.

The bed was similar – it was made of bracken, we used to cut it out of the Forest. Mat grass we used to call it. Some of that, and straw, and we used to tuck it back in with a little bit of stick, with a tick over the top of it, and mum used to put coats, anything, down underneath us to keep the water from coming under. Used to dig a little drain around the tent. That's the bed we used to have because we couldn't get the beds on the ponies and carts, so make it too heavy for the horses to pull and take up too much room.

On the end of the tent, on the front of the tent where we used to go in and out, we used to make some rods up like a tepee and we used to make a fire in the centre of it. Mainly we used to keep the fire going slowly – built it up during the day, get a nice lot of coals inside of it and then we used to keep it nice and warm. Better than any house. We used to live in the winter in the snow and the frost, things like that. We done the cooking on there. We used to stick a big iron bar down in – we called it a kiddle crane – there is one out in my garden now, we used to get it made from the blacksmith. With a hook thing on the top of it, we put the pot on there, or the kiddle, or get a couple of bricks if we could get hold of them, put them down along the side, put a saucepan on there and make a stew or something.

I went to school. I went sometimes a week at one place, fortnight at the other, sometimes a month. When we used to travel around we used to be close to a school and then we used to go to school. Come in with two or three different families and their children went to school. The village children used to get jealous of us and they used to go and tell the School Board – bloke that goes around now if you had a day off, school attendant. They used to find out where we lived and then they used to come up and see my mother and father and we had to go to school.

In the summertime we used to go out in the fields, working. We didn't have no school then. We used to bide there for about a week, a fortnight, never had time to send us to school. We used to do tater picking-up, strawberry picking, hoeing, pulling the doubles with my mother when I was small, very small – just leaving one plant in a place. Dad used to go along with the hoe, chop them out and he used to leave one plant, take the weeds out. All sorts of things we used to do,- helping my father basket making, go out with him rag and boning, in wintertime that was. Help him make baskets, mats, doormats, saucepan lids, pot lids…oh, my father could put his hand nearly to everything and he taught me my trade, what I knows. Jack- of- all- trades and master of none!"

Even though the accounts of Gypsy life given in the New Forest by Louisa and Tom are more than fifty years apart, the similarities of lifestyle and employment are strikingly similar. Another similarity is that Louisa and Tom ended up living in houses, as did Andy "Frustrated Commoner" who was also interviewed by Mike Turner:

"Our family can be traced back in the New Forest, right back to the seventeen hundreds, as a travelling family in the Forest – yes, as in Gypsies. Most of my family, my relations, still live at Thorney Hill, which is where my father came from. He came from the Gypsy camp at Thorney Hill to the Gypsy camp which used to be just up the road here, sort of half a mile, in the Forest. It's just a clump of trees in the middle of the Forest which we all know as 'the Gypsy camp'. When the Gypsies were re-housed my family were re-housed to the cottage where I was born. I'm one of twelve children so we were quite a large family. I'm sort of the outcast of the family. I've gone off and done my own thing".

In the final section of his book – "The Visitors" – Mike Taylor interviews some tourists at the New Forest campsites. He talks to some campers in a "small caravan on a campsite, deep in the woodland" and also to "an extended family in two caravans". The bitter irony is that there are now many more campsites and caravans in the New Forest than there ever were Gypsy tents and vardos. The Holmsley campsite I stayed at in 2003 was massive, and could accommodate hundreds of people.

Mike Taylor talked to Derek, a campsite warden, who explained that "the big campsites get filled on the Friday evening". Mike asked Derek "Were you here when the New Age travellers came to this part of the Forest?" Derek remembered it well: "There was ninety or a hundred vehicles. Then on the Friday and Saturday and Sunday nights they were joined by the part time hippies out of the outlying areas.... They vacated at two o'clock in the afternoon on the Monday and they didn't give us one iota of trouble...They actually left the site quite clear – they put all their rubbish in black bags and stacked it."

Despite causing no trouble and tidying up their litter (by contrast, "the general public can be very, very untidy") Derek could not "have these sort of people coming onto the campsite because they are not people who want to pay camping fees." Also, "these sort of people" made the caravanners on the campsite feel "nervous". The same thing happened to the Gypsies, who were the New Forest's original visitors, campers and caravanners. They started to make people feel "nervous" and did not want to have their lifestyle curbed by the increasing bureaucracy of the Forest wardens. First they were herded into compounds and later into camps and council houses. Their freedom to travel around and work in the Forest was taken away. And much else was lost besides. This sense of loss is described by Mike Turner:

"Every time I visit the Forest, an old rhyme keeps going round in my head. It was composed by 'Anon.' in the times when the common lands of England were being enclosed during the eighteenth and nineteenth centuries. Nothing of that sort is happening in 1998 of course, but yet I feel a great sense of loss, of deprivation, as if someone had stolen something from me. I cannot put this clearly into words, so I must let the unknown writer of this doggerel speak for me:

The law doth punish man or woman
That steals the goose from off the common;
But lets the greater felon loose
That steals the common from the goose.

Valediction
Brian Vesey- Fitzgerald can trace this sense of loss back to 1947: "Looking back, I think that there can be no doubt that the most important date in the recent history of the Gypsies of Britain, perhaps the most important date in all their long history, was the day in November 1947 when the Report of the New Forest Committee was published." The Committee was appointed in April 1946 "to investigate the state and condition of the New Forest and, having due regard to existing rights and interests, to recommend such measures as they consider desirable and necessary for adjusting the Forest to modern requirements." During the course of their investigations they visited the Gypsy compounds and, in their Report, commented upon them.

The compound system was started in 1926. Gypsies who previously could camp anywhere in the Forest for up to 48 hours now had to live in one of seven permanent compounds, including one at Thorney Hill. There was no general outcry by the residents in the Forest against the Gypsies, but there was what Vesey-Fitzgerald calls a change of climate. "For the first time there was a lack of understanding of the Gypsy way of life, a complete lack of sympathy with it. Not among the Commoners…And not among the old established gentry of the Forest nor among the old established villagers and tradesmen…But among a new type which settled in the New Forest after the end of the First World War.

The compound system interfered with the rhythm of the Gypsy way of life. Gypsies live in family groups and are not gregarious. The compounds forced them to live with other Gypsies and this led to bickering and trouble between families. The compounds did not allow the Gypsy to maintain his regular circuit of work and so his business suffered. Faced with the compound system, some packed up and moved out of the Forest altogether. For those who stayed, within ten years the compounds were being used as a matter of convenience rather than of necessity and there were a number of Gypsy families camping in the Forest.

During the Second World War the New Forest Gypsies were rounded up and put into five compounds. A harsher, less tolerant, world was to be born of the Second World War, as evidenced by the 1947 Report which talked of the New Forest Gypsies still living in the "Stone Age". The Gypsies were effectively put on trial in this Report (without being allowed to defend themselves) and found guilty of a crime which they were not responsible for (they had been herded into the compounds which had no water or sanitary arrangements.)

The Report suggested that Gypsy children were outnumbering the children of local residents in some Forest schools. As Vesey-Fitzgerald pointed out, the total Gypsy population in the Forest at the time was 411 men, women and children. And none of the village school teachers was asked to give evidence to the Committee. "Nobody wanted to listen to those who were prepared to speak up for the Gypsies."

Despite the Committee's opinion – "the simple solution is to remove all Gypsies" – the compounds remained. A better solution would have been to allow the Gypsies to resume their ancient custom of camping where they wished in the open Forest. There was never any realisation that the solitary camp of a Gypsy family, moved every 48 hours, constituted no danger, was more sanitary, and infinitely healthier in every way than the compound.

Although nothing changed immediately as a result of the 1947 Report, almost everything that has happened since to Gypsies in England and Wales stems directly from this Report. This was the first government report for many years to present the Gypsies as a serious problem and to create a hostile attitude towards Gypsies. "The Report set the tone for officialdom for years to come". It also aroused local and national interest in the compounds and Gypsies which reached far beyond the Forest. "Gypsies were now, as never before news". And the news was usually bad.

Another major contributing factor "was that the pattern of life everywhere in the world was changing. And by far the most important feature of this changing pattern was speed. In the last resort it has been speed that, in England, has wrecked the Gypsy way of life". This speed of change, combined with the growing levels of intolerance and bureaucracy had a disastrous effect on the Gypsy life style. Increases in the standard of living lead to Gypsies being regarded with contempt, as inferior beings and dirty people.

Between the wars – as evidenced by Patrick McEvoy's *The Gorse and the Briar* – there was still a generally tolerant attitude of the village towards the Gypsies. Any complaints then came mainly from the well to do middle class. This became much more noticeable after the war. Suburbia absorbed the villages and introduced suburban ways of life and values. If a Gypsy family appeared on the edge of this sort of suburbia it was lowering the tone of the neighbourhood. Gypsies were moved on, and kept moving by a police force which had also changed. This harsher, less tolerant, England is described in Dominic Reeve's *Smoke in the Lanes* and *No Place Like Home*.

According to the government survey *Gypsies and Other Travellers* (1965) the most common complaints against Gypsies were that they were dirty and untidy. But these were the complaints of town bred people. By contrast, Ralph Wightman, who was country born and bred, had nothing but positive comments to make about Gypsies in his book *Abiding Things*: "One class of people who know all the old rights of way are the Gypsies...They very seldom do any real harm, and they are better than most campers as far is litter is concerned."

The irony is that Gypsies were disliked because they were nomadic. But the solution was to move them on! Constant complaints about Gypsies, particularly in southern and south eastern England, helped to establish an atmosphere hostile to Gypsies. While the people complained the actual attack came from the Town Hall or from the Council Offices. Local Authorities maintained that the problem was essentially a national one. The Government maintained that these were matters for the Local Authorities themselves. As a result Local Authorities with a Gypsy problem reverted to the words of the 1947 Report – "the simple solution is to remove all the Gypsies as soon as possible to some place." The situation became much worse for the Gypsies when a Conservative government was elected in 1951. This government had no intention of becoming involved with any Gypsy problem and the atmosphere became colder and harsher for the Gypsies.

From 1951 onwards much greater use was made of Acts of Parliament by Local Authorities with a Gypsy community on their doorstep. From now on, time after time, we find a distinction being drawn by the Local Authority between the "true Romani" and the people being harassed. This is a return to the language of the 1947 Report concerning "the true Romany strain". As Vesey-Fitzgerald said, such a distinction is nonsense. "The Romani blood has always been mixed in some measure with that of the local gorgio population."

In the New Forest the Ringwood and Fordingbridge Rural District Council very early started on a policy of resettlement, moving families from the compounds to council house accommodation. In *Dromengro* Sven Berlin vividly described the effect of this resettlement on some Gypsies. The process of resettlement was a lengthy one. Over a period of time Hampshire housed all the Gypsies. In the words of Vesey-Fitzgerald

"The Gypsy is being absorbed or, rather, he is entering the community of his own wish. The long history of the Gypsies of Britain is coming to an end."

Pateman = Pateran ?
"Gypsies left signs in the road for each other, known as the Patrin, usually in the form of an elongated cross made out of twigs, to show which way they had gone. Other Gypsies could tell by how old the twigs were and from what type of wood etc., who had passed and where they were going. They also left signs on gateposts to houses and farms to inform others of the type of reception they might expect." (Paultons)

This Gypsy custom of *Strewing the Pateran* (or Patrin) is depicted in a painting by Amelia Goddard and decribed on the Hampshire Gypsies website: "This secret code is the patrin, a system of signs left on the road to give a clear message to other travellers. Often the signs consist only of a handful of grass, a notch on a tree, or a cross drawn on the ground. But from these the Gypsy can tell which direction has been taken, how many vans or families are in the group and how far ahead they are on the road.

Sometimes symbols are left on a village wall or at a particular farm to tell other Gypsies whether the people are friendly or hostile. Among New Forest Gypsies the patrin attained a considerable degree of sophistication and individuality. Bent sticks, for instance, indicated travellers on foot; straight sticks were used to indicate vans; branched twigs or a spray of gorse showed a family with children.

The patrin varied, of course, from family to family, so that the amount of information contained in the signs was limited to one particular tribe. This was the case for most families of New Forest and Hampshire Gypsies"

My New Forest Gypsy ancestors have left me clues and signs by which I can follow them – Gypsy ballads, newspaper stories and names on gravestones. Romany and Traveller family history is the modern day equivalent of Strewing the Pateran. I also find it interesting to note that by replacing the letter "m" in my surname with the letter "r" it is possible to convert Pateman into Pateran – just a coincidence or yet another clue to my past?

2. Gypsies Halting by the Ling

"It is four o'clock on Magpie Green, one of the many lawns which wind in and out of the holly-shelters on Thorney Hill. Holmsley lies away in the distance. The day, with its

*"Queenly crimson deep in the heather,
And diamonds of the dew at morn
Flashing their rainbow drops together,"*

has already begun for this group of Gypsies who have just un-harnessed the horses from their three caravans, which loom red and yellow and tawny brown to the still misty grey. The water has to be fetched for breakfast soon, and the fires lit; you can hear the high-pitched voice of the chablos, and the soft voice of the dai, hushing the betichavi in her arms, her dark face turned to the dawn; you can hear the awakening whispers of the wind in the heath,

*"For thee and for me, my child,
Wandering folk and poor,
There are jewels of price on meadow and moor,
When the wind blows wild"*

The 1869 Ordnance Survey map of Thorney Hill features Magpie Green, Cross Ways, Thorny Hill Holms, Jopp's Plantation, Poors Common and Hill Farm. Thorney Hill Holmes – the holly wood where the Gypsies lived - was much more extensive in 1869 than it is today. This map also shows a number of brick fields and kilns, which are clues to Thorney Hill's more industrial past.

The 1896 Ordnance Survey Map of Thorney Hill shows the Methodist Chapel. The 1907 Map shows All Saints Church and the school. The 2002 Ordnance Survey map shows Thorney Hill as it is today – in many ways it has changed very little since the map of 1869. Features such as Magpie Green, Cross Ways, Thorny Hill Holms, Jopp's Plantation, Poors Common and Hill Farm still appear on the map. One difference is Holmsley Camp, on the site of the former airfield.

Thorney Hill
Thorney Hill formed part of the enormous Parish of Christchurch until 1875 when it was included in the Parish of Bransgore. Thorney Hill became part of the Parish of Christchurch East in 1894. It returned to the parish of Bransgore in 1974.

Thorney Hill This, That and T'Other by M.W. Penfold combines a good general history of Thorney Hill with some "interesting memories of this area; folk who have known hard times and how to survive". Penfold's "captured memories" are dedicated to her late husband Frank "who was proud of Thorney Hill". Many people were willing to share their memories with Mrs Penfold: "It is to these friends I owe this book, and hope it will be appreciated by many, as a reminder of how things have changed in this century."

"Holly is mentioned in the Domesday Book at Holmsley. In the earliest records of the New Forest made by King John 1199-1216, the landmarks on the boundary at

Thorney Hill are given as the mound, later called Eversley, the old name for the intersection of two very old tracks.

Later it was known as Crossways. Eversley was often muddled with another village of the same name in the North of the county, so to make sure the visiting Vicar went to the right place, it was changed to Thorney Hill, possibly coming from thorns of gorse or blackthorn. In 1983 Thorney Hill was officially put on the map with its own signpost."

The hay season was an important one in the farming calendar, as the live-stock's existence depended on it during the winter: "Local farmers would be very dependent on the casual labour from the Forest dwellers, as many fields in the area needed hoeing or weeding. If the field was large, and it was a good growing season, no sooner had it been done, than it needed doing again."

The original small cob and thatch cottage, later known as the "off licence", was built in the 1780s and occupied by the Hann family for at least fifty years prior to 1896. They added a bakery to the premises. In 1896 Richard Pitt rented the shop from Strong and Company, making use of the bakery to sell bread and dough cakes, but only at the weekends. As well as beer and drinks, they did a good trade in coal, cattle and horse feeds, supplying many local farmers:

"An off licence / shop was opened in 1896. Maurice Pitt bought it in 1962 and built up its trade considerably, supplying everything a small community needed, as there were by now a number of council houses. Some of the occupants had been re-housed from the Forest, and they would visit the shop two or three times a day, purchasing supplies they needed at the time. Fridges and freezers were not common necessities then."

In the late 1800s and early 1900s the cottages built on Thorney Hill were made of a mixture of mud, clay and heather with water added, making it ready for moulding for the walls.

The Story of Thorney Hill, by Ruth Lavender, wife of John Lavender (who was for many years curator at Christchurch's Red House Museum) is another font of local knowledge. She has meticulously researched the story of this strange area, halfway between Bransgore and Burley and between the New Forest and the Avon Valley:

"Gypsies have had a long association with Thorney Hill. The first Methodist Chapel was built in 1864 but destroyed by fire in 1875. A good Sunday school met in the chapel and Gypsy mothers as well as others brought their children for baptism. In the 1870's two or three children a month were being baptised at the chapel, and many of them were Gypsies." Several of them were Patemans.

"I was told of a travelling Minister who would probably preach at a Chapel, then go visiting the Forest people. He was keen that they should be legally married, but they had brought up a family together and didn't see the need for a piece of paper. Some of the children kept father's surname, and others mother's name, which must have caused problems at school!" (Penfold)

Thorney Hill school opened in 1892, to teach the growing number of children living in and around the village: "Numerous Gypsy children attended Thorney Hill school and later Bransgore School and Twynham Comprehensive in Christchurch. Phoebe Burslem was one time headmistress at Thorney Hill school. Her work with the Gypsy children was unusual and commanded great respect. She handed out real money to them to learn to handle it through play, and she started – and got the money for – annual visits for the entire school to Bournemouth pantomime. In 1946 Miss Burslem lectured to the students at Salisbury Training College on her Gypsy school, an event recalled with enthusiasm by one of her hearers forty years later." (Lavender)

"It is difficult to state exactly the number of children in attendance, as this fluctuated according to the time of year. In the summer many families took to the roads in search of casual work. Travellers' children were required by law to attend the school nearest to where the parents were working, for a certain number of days each year, except for hop picking which coincided with holidays anyway." (Penfold)

Jane and Charles Broomfield came to Thorney Hill about 1900, and were able to buy most of the land available at that time. They either bought or built cottages in School Road, Forest Road, and down the main road towards Bransgore, on the west side. The cob and thatch cottage in School Road owned by them was used as a shop, to supply the villagers with groceries of all kinds. Their son Bertie Broomfield married Mary Jane Pateman in 1904.

There used to be four wells on the Hill: Pennell's well by the crossroads; Benny's well between School Road and Valley Lane; one below the Chapel, and one in the Paddock on School Lane. It was not until about the 1930's that the main water was piped to the Hill.

There used to be about a dozen or so farmers on the Hill, who made a living by keeping cows, as far as people can remember. A byre or a long low-roofed shed would often be built at the back of the cottage, in which the cows could be individually tied for milking by hand. They would then be turned out on to the Forest to wander at will, finding natural herbage to eat.

In 1906 a small club was built alongside the Burley Road so the men of the village could gather for a gossip. Later a drinks licence was obtained and *The Drum and Monkey* became a Working Men's Social Club. It cost one shilling a year to belong.

All Saints Church was built in 1906 by Lord and Lady Manners of Avon Tyrrell, in memory of their daughter: "Miss Hay (who at one time lived at Thorney Hill House and Tyrell's Ford) played the organ and trained a choir at All Saints. She was wonderful with children and at distributions of oranges etc to Gypsy children at Christmas it was she who knew all the children well enough to forestall attempts to join the queue again and get a second share." (Lavender)

"Later on so many Gypsies were buried in the churchyard of All Saints that it was sometimes called the 'Gypsy church'. Standing round the graveside, packed with mourning relatives and friends from the travelling community a small, squeaky voice was heard to ask, 'What be they a-doing to Uncle Toby now?' 'Burying the bugger, casn't see!' " (Penfold)

There was a small garage just in the vicinity of Thorney Hill. The owners used it to supply petrol by the can to Avon Tyrrell, delivering it by horse and cart. They were also the only taxi service to and from Holmsley Station.

Brick Kilns
In the latter part of the 1800s Thorney Hill had a thriving brick industry and fuel was required to keep the brick kilns going: "The travellers camped on the forest would be employed to cut bundles of gorse and twigs for kindling. Coal and perhaps turf would then be used to keep a constant heat. This needed a man on duty day and night for about three to four days. There used to be a ventilation shaft left at each end, as the heat would be terrific. The bricks took several days to cool before being loaded on the wagon and carted off to their destination. Most carters used to sit on the shafts and drive the horse from the side." (Penfold)

There were five brick kilns in the area as far as we know at the beginning of 1900. One was at the corner of School Road; two down Brick Lane, naturally taking its name from the site; and two owned by Benny Broomfield just above Walkers Garage. There were a few in Burnt House Lane and Bransgore:

"By the middle of the nineteenth century there were several houses and considerable activity at Thorney Hill. Bricks were in demand for building the new town of Bournemouth. Brick Kiln Bottom had acquired its name by 1852, and on the 1869 Ordnance Survey Map three brick fields and two kilns are shown in the north-west and two more brickworks, one on each side of Burley Road also with kilns; the big clay pits are still visible from the road.

Brickyards were small and the land and buildings were commonly rented by their operators. Diggers protected their feet with an iron guard strapped over the boot, and gorse was used for firing (sometimes cut by the men and rolled into faggots by the women). This local industry continued into the twentieth century." (Lavender)

In the early 1900s the small village of Bournemouth was largely owned by the Cooper-Dean family. People from the towns suddenly discovered the desirability of owning a property by the seaside. The small village grew by leaps and bounds and Thorney Hill brick makers were hard put to keep up with the demand. The sand and gravel in this area is of a particularly good quality and much sought after.

Brick kilns were originally built on the site of a good clay bed. Sand had to be mixed with the clay before being put into moulds. The moulds would be levelled off and cut with a piece of wire to the right size. A kiln was built like a small room with a doorway in one end. When the bricks had dried, they were loaded on a flat bottomed wheelbarrow and stacked in rows in the kiln. A narrow passage was left each side, connected with archways built in the walls. The firing was pushed in these vents, then lit and sealed with clay. There could be as many as 32,000 bricks in a kiln at one firing.

For more information about the brick industry see *Of Bricks and Brickworks by* "Rambler" in *Nova Foresta Magazine* (Autumn/Winter 2003/04): "Towards the latter part of the 19th century there were about 100 to 150 brickworks in Hampshire, most of the bricks being hand made. In the New Forest area nearly all closed in the 1930s.

Thorney Hill near Bransgore had a number of brickyards in the 19th century. Sand and gravel in the area is of an especially good quality. Many Thorney Hill bricks were used in building the new town of Bournemouth."

Holmsley South Airfield
Holmsley South Aerodrome was built between 1941 and 1942, and opened on 1st September still incomplete, to accommodate reinforcements to 19 Group RAF Coastal Command during "Operation Torch". Domestic sites and dispersals were still incomplete when the RAF personnel started arriving. The planes which flew from here included Liberator, Halifax and Wellington bombers.

Early in 1944 the station was transferred to 10 Group for fighter operations in preparation for D Day support operations. Spitfire, Typhoon, Mosquito and Mustang fighters were joined by Dakota, C-54 and Warwick transport aircraft. General Eisenhower visited Holmsley Aerodrome to send the American airmen off for the D Day landings.

After the Battle of Britain Show in September 1946 the station was reduced to care and maintenance status on 16 October 1946. Eventually it was closed completely. In the sixties the land reverted to the Forestry Commission who later removed most of the runways, and taxiways, returning the land to the Forest.

A comprehensive "history of a New Forest airfield in war and peace" is told by Leslie White in *The Holmsley Story*: "Geographically, Holmsley South was reckoned to be suitable for this purpose. It lay well within an area bounded by the villages of Bransgore, Burley, Wootton and Hinton together with the village and Gypsy encampment at Thorney Hill.

Some of the locals worked permanently on the station until its closure in November 1946. One of these was Harry Coker (more usually 'Old Coke') who soon found that running the station piggery, with its considerable perks, a much better proposition than hawking clothes-pegs around the neighbourhood."

An article on the *Holmsley Airfield Memorial* by Anne Biffin appeared in the *Nova Foresta Magazine* (Autumn/Winter 2003/04): "A splendid white memorial set with a huge propeller and twelve plaques, one for each New Forest airfield. A time capsule containing a piece of wreckage from a Messerschmitt shot down over Milford on Sea, and part of a US Liberator found at Beaulieu Heath, a pilot's helmet and other WW2 mementos are encased in the rear of the memorial. The whole area is surrounded by gold tipped black railings. The Union flag and the Stars and Stripes fluttered on either side of the memorial which faces the old runway, now returned to grass."

The former airfield is now a well established caravan site run by the Forestry Commission. On my visit to the area in 2003 I bought two post cards: one shows a Gypsy family outside their Bender tent in the New Forest, taken from a late nineteenth century collection of J.G. Short glass plates held by the New Forest Ninth Century Trust. The other postcard is an aerial view of Holmsley campsite. There is a bitter irony in these two postcards: one shows a way of life, generations old, which was wiped out by legislation and intolerance; the other depicts the modern yearning for that same freedom of life on the move, sleeping under canvas, and cooking on an open fire.

Smuggling
Penfold includes some extracts from *Smuggling in Hants and Dorset* by G. Morley: "Beech House, standing deep in the woods of Bransgore, had its own ice house. This was a most useful delivery place for smugglers on their way to the Forest. During the Reign of Terror in France 1789 when hundreds of the noblemen and women were being executed, smugglers would be paid by them for a passage to England. In return these people would be persuaded to carry contraband hidden in their clothes. Beech House was used as a refuge for these French aristocrats.

One noble family, unable to get away altogether, heard of a young Captain with a fast cutter. They offered him a large sum of money to take their daughter to England. They gave him half, and promised him the rest when he arrived at Beech House. They were delayed by strong winds round Guernsey, by which time the handsome Captain had fallen in love with the beautiful French girl. When they reached Christchurch harbour they were deeply involved, and the whole crew was talking about it. They tied up at dead of night and a trusty friend of the Captain's was sent ahead with a letter, to prepare the girl's relations for her arrival.

The Chief Riding Officer for the Customs was on patrol next day, along the quay so they were unable to leave the shelter of the boat. This was long enough for mischief to work, for the messenger had not only told the French at Beech House of the lady's arrival, but also the Captain's sweetheart! She lived in the Forest at Thorney Hill, and had Gypsy blood in her veins. So successful was her jealousy aroused she flung herself on her pony and made straight for No.10 Bridge Street and told the Revenue men where the Captain was. They galloped up to Bransgore, only to be met by the smugglers hightailing back to their ship. They rode through the Customs men, but didn't realise till they reached the open sea that their Captain had a gunshot wound in his back, which discouraged him from returning."

Characters
Ned Penfold made a lasting impression on some folk he met: " 'A striking character, tall and handsome with flashing black eyes, and a gold earring in his ear', recollects Mr Lawford from Burley. Ned bought three cottages in the Paddock, now School Lane, from Mr Clough, who sent his agent to collect the money. He didn't realise it would be in gold sovereigns, so he had to ride his bicycle back to Burley and return with a horse and cart.

A regular visitor to the Forest was a man from The Church Army, who would visit church halls, or schools with a magic lantern show. He owned one of the old Romany caravans, which was pulled by a black and white horse. One evening his show took place in a barn. When one lad, Barty by name, came to leave, he quietly smuggled a sleeping bantam out under his felt hat. Unfortunately half way home across the Forest the little hen woke up, and discovered its roosting place was moving! Barty realising he'd be in serious trouble with his parents, quickly returned the bantam to the barn.

Mischief was one thing, but stealing was a different thing altogether. These travellers had a strict code of honesty. The local baker used to deliver bread to the folk living in the area of White's bushes, he was never owed for a loaf of bread even.

Knife grinding was a skill few possessed, yet many needed, and the man from The Hill was well known in the areas round about. While he was out grinding, his wife would be making rush baskets at home. One of these, given as a wedding present to the local Doctor is a much valued possession.

There was an honest story told me; by one who shared his childhood with the travellers. He was on his way home through the Forest bushes, one dark night, when the heavens opened and thunder crashed overhead. Suddenly a flash of lightning lit the path in front of the boys. There beside the path a white apparition was standing under a tree. Petrified, they fled back to the tents, sure they had seen The Devil! When the storm died down, they all returned to investigate. There, was a white donkey, tethered, quietly browsing the leaves on branches above his head! No wonder the path is called Devils Walk! After 70 years this is still imprinted on the man's memory."

The following snippet appeared in the *Bournemouth Echo* in 1979: "Brashfield Country Fair. Delighted villagers at Thorney Hill were asked to play their part in a unique Hampshire Country Fair. Mr J Saunders, the craft fair organiser, wanted the folk who could remember the secret skills of the travelling people to get together. He secured a promise from a packed Village Hall meeting that the villagers would come on June 2nd and 3rd to demonstrate the ways of making clothes pegs, paper flowers and other traditional skills. The two-day event included sheep shearing, hurdle and basket making, pottery, and the presence of a Romany caravan."

The Manners Family
The Manners family are descended directly from the Dukes of Rutland whose own ancestor was standard bearer at Hastings for William the Conqueror. John, the 3rd Lord Manners, was known as "Hoppy" because of his characteristic walk. He was also a skilful horseman and once road his horse Seaman to a win in the Grand National and it is alleged that the family seat at Avon Tyrrell was built on the proceeds. Lady Constance Manners was known as Con.

In 1890 William Lethaby was chosen by Lord Manners to build the house at Avon Tyrrell, where his wife's family, the Fanes, held a good deal of land. In fact Lady Constance Manners (Constance Fane) was born in a house at Avon Tyrrell. The new house was completed in 1892. All Saints Church, Thorney Hill, is also built on land owned by the Fane family

Lord and Lady Manners were closely associated with members of a group called the Souls, which contained aristocrats and famous people who were friends of the young Lord Curzon. It is not known how they came to be called the Souls but it was alleged that they were very introspective and always examining their souls. They seemed to share a strong, somewhat "unorthodox" religious bond as well. This group of over 50 people met in each other's houses from the Duke of Sutherland's castle to Avon Tyrrell, where the Manners lived. Only the Great War brought it to an end in the tragedy of so many of them being killed or ruined. They were great patrons of artists and craftsmen such as Detmar Blow, Eric Gill, Sir Bertram MacKennal and Phoebe Traquair.

I am very thankful to Canon Patrick Elkins, the Vicar of All Saints (1967-2004), for allowing me to use his unpublished notes on the history of the Manners Family and All Saints Church: "Con and Hoppy were not 'souls' though they knew and were friendly with a number of this group. To be a genuine 'soul' you would have to have been present at a particular dinner evening hosted by Lord Curzon (later the Marquis of Curzon). You could be an honorary soul – unofficially. There were a few of these. Those special dinner guests were 'The Lang' and their children made up 'The Coterie'. This group was I think unique in going beyond the initiators to the next generation."

All Saints Church
All Saints Church, Thorney Hill, is a Chapel of Ease to St Mary's in Bransgore and is open weekly for public worship. It is not a private chapel, as was the rumour, but built for everyone in that area. The local Gypsy community has always claimed it as their own, and return for baptisms, marriages and burials. The church is listed Grade One – only 0.5% of listed buildings are so graded.

Canon Elkins: "This church was built in 1906 in memory of Mary Christine, daughter of Lord and Lady Manners, who died in 1904, in India as a result of a cholera outbreak – she was seventeen. The cherubs on the door are alleged to be likenesses of Mary Christine.

The site was provided in the 1880s by Lady Constance and her sister for a church for the local people who included Romany families from the Forest brought in by a local brick-maker to tend their kilns at night. Thereafter they settled and now regard the church as their "family" church, returning to it for special occasions."

Detmar Blow
The architect was Detmar Blow who built All Saints between 1904-6, when he was about 37 years old. It was as far as we know his only church. He was "taken up" by John Ruskin who encouraged him to work first hand in the materials he would use when designing buildings. As a young man he was also closely associated with William Morris (Arts and Crafts Movement founder and Christian Socialist) and he designed the funeral cart which bore Morris to his grave.

All Saints is unusually a North-South orientated building rather than East-West. It is designed with Arts and Crafts principles in mind – to be lit with candles only and with the smoke from the heating system directed out through the tower. By church law the altar should be made of wood, but Blow used Italian marble. This was overlooked at the dedication of the chapel by Edward Ryle, Bishop of Winchester, on 18 October 1906. It is thought that the altar is a copy of that situated in King's College Chapel in Cambridge.

The church cost £5,601 to build, which included the price of £2,473 for the beautiful white stone from Caen in France. The cross and candlesticks on the altar were designed by Bainsbridge & Reynolds of Clapham. Despite being decorated with amethyst, they cost £45.

National Trust Magazine: "Sometimes it seems that it has never been more difficult to be upwardly mobile. In the second half of the nineteenth century, meteoric rises appear to have come ten a penny. One such was Detmar Blow, the son of a shellac, tea and coffee merchant in Mincing Lane who was somehow able to become an architect, marry aristocracy – and design buildings for absolutely the best set.

Perhaps Detmar was helped by his rather remarkable name: his brother, who was blessed with the somehow much less interesting moniker of Sydney, wrote: 'Detmar always had rigid ideas for raising the family up! Up! UP!' He was descended from John Blow, the famous organist and 17th century composer for James II, William and Mary and Queen Anne.

He had some amazing mentors, including some of the greatest in the Arts and Crafts movement. John Ruskin first discovered him sketching in Abbeville Cathedral. He more or less adopted him, taking him off to the Italian Alps in between intermittent bouts of madness.

Yet Blow seems to have been lovable, rather than a manipulative social climber. A man of 'singularly good looks', the ladies loved him. Winifred, second daughter of the Hon. Hamilton Tollemache, married the man she found drawing in her garden, in a Gypsy caravan.

Society thought the couple wildly eccentric. Mrs Blow did everything herself for the children, breast feeding them and even washing them. They weren't kept out of sight in a nursery, because there wasn't one. They weren't even beaten when naughty, the extraordinary idea was that they should learn by example and gentle persuasion. A family friend, Neville Lytton, described their childcare system as 'a period of monstrous anarchy between the years of five and ten.'

For a time, before they all found it too embarrassing, the servants ate with them in the kitchen. 'Mr and Mrs regard themselves as the servants of all their dependents; children, domestics, farmers and labourers,' Lytton observed.

There were no daily prayers, but folk ideas were observed as an almost holy ritual. The household would sing a folk song before work, and have country dancing after tea, with the servants joining in. Blow was a passionate advocate of craftsmanship, and gave up his conventional architect's training to apprentice himself to a Newcastle builder. When it came to restoring a building like The Old Post Office at Tintagel, he was the obvious choice.

Blow became an agent for the dreadful Bendor, the self indulgent playboy and 2nd Duke of Westminster (one of the world's richest men) whose yacht, *Flying Cloud*, Blow had designed like a Queen Anne house." Canon Elkins: "Bendor was really Bend'or, referring to his coat of arms which includes the "bend or" = bar in gold. So Bendor was his nickname. Bendor got bored with Blow and he was dismissed in the 1920s on a trumped up charge. The disgrace drove him insane." Blow also designed the Grosvenor House Hotel and was responsible for much of the redevelopment of that area of London.

Sir Bertram MacKennal

Lord and Lady Manners' son, the Hon. John Manners, Grenadier Guards, was killed in action on 1 September 1914, aged 21, in the decisive battle of Mons. A memorial of him, a reclining bronze effigy designed by Sir Bertram MacKennal was placed in the church in 1917. The wording of the memorial and that of the tablet for Mary Christine was suggested by the Hon. Sir John Fortescue, military historian and sometime librarian of Windsor castle.

Canon Elkins: "MacKennal was an Australian and a student and close friend of the greatest sculptor since Michaelangelo – Auguste Rodin. MacKennal did famous statues of Queen Victoria and Edward VII. He also designed the obverse (head) of the coinage for the reign of King George V. The obverse design carried "B.M." initials on the raised neck which is a singular honour granted by George V who was a personal friend. You can just see it with a powerful eye glass."

Eric Gill

The lettering of the memorial to John Manners – and to his sister Mary Christine - were personally cut by the renowned sculptor, Eric Gill, who was responsible for reviving the essential form of Roman lettering. Gill also carved the angels on the memorial to John Manners. It is very telling of the sadness endured that the angels are prostrate with grief, which is an unusual depiction of them.

Gill was twenty-four when he began work at All Saints. The Mary Christine inscription has in it an error "honestly owned":

"This chapel was raised by Lord John Manners & Constance his wife to the Glory of God in memory of Mary Christine their daughter who was called from them in the eighteenth year of her earthly life to worship him as they trust. For ever in a temple not made with hands. She died at Bangalore in India 15 Feb 1904 & lies buried at Clovelly in Devonshire."

"To the beloved memory of a lieutenant in His Majesty's Grenadier Guards who fell in victorious combat with the German infantry among the woodlands of Villers Cotterets in the north of France & lies in one grave with an hundred British soldiers his comrades of a devoted rearguard at peace in the silence of the forest. John Manners born Jan 6. 1892, killed Sep 1. 1914".

"We fought for England in the war 1914-1918 and wounded and sick found at Avon Tyrrell healing and a home. This stone is set here in token of our love and gratitude. Four hundred officers of the New Zealand Expeditionary Force."

These three inscriptions by Gill are nationally listed as his finest work in this style. The church also contains a listing of "Men serving in His Majesty's Forces in the war from this parish" and an embroidered depiction of All Saints.

Phoebe Traquair

The Manners family were to suffer another loss in 1920 with the death of Lady Constance. As a memorial to her, the windows in the apse above the altar were blocked up and a mural was painted by the Irish artist Phoebe Traquair, a friend of the Manners family. Traquair (1852-1936) was well known for her work in the Edinburgh

School of Song. She was also famous as the first woman artist to be elected to the Royal Scottish Academy in 1920 – the year in which she started this, her last major work, aged 68 years.

Like Michaelangelo, Traquair painted on scaffolding and wrote during the work that she was often very uncomfortable and weary. She studied and used the methods of Leonardo da Vinci. The subdued colours and restrained nature of the mural – compared with earlier richer, more triumphant and confident work - fits in well with the theme of sorrow and regret and the "pity of war", at the same time affirming Te Deum – "We praise thee, O God". The domed roof is of Christ in Glory. Here a very youthful Jesus is surrounded by children and young people, taken from photographs of local school children in 1922.

The main central panel portrays the New Forest – landscape, trees, birds and flowers. The roof-line of Avon Tyrrell House can be seen peeping above the trees on the horizon. Also in view are the Waterloo Clump of Scots firs planted to celebrate the Battle of Waterloo. These were destroyed by the hurricane of 1990.

The subject of the mural is a Te Deum for "All sorts and conditions of men" and shows not only friends and members of the family but also notable people of the last century. Traquair liked to paint real people in her paintings and so, though unfortunately some names are lost, the identity of many of them is known:

Lady Constance Manners (1861-1920) – the mural is a fitting tribute to a lady who had a major effect on many of her friends, including Frances Horner, Raymond Asquith and Duff Cooper. Lady Manners suffered much personal tragedy and was destined to die at the comparatively young age of 59.

John Manners (1892-1914) – Lord and Lady Manners oldest son, killed in the Mons Retreat. An entry from the diaries of Lady Cynthia Asquith (daughter in law of Prime Minister Asquith) tells us "Avon (Tyrrell) was a frame for John" which was now empty and meaningless.

Francis Henry Lord Manners (1897-1972) – Francis succeeded to the title of Fourth Baron Manners when his father Lord John died I 1927. He married Mary Edith Cecil (1900-1994, daughter of Lord William Cecil, Bishop of Exeter (second son of Lord Salisbury, Queen Victoria's first Prime Minister).

Raymond Asquith – the son of Prime Minister Herbert Asquith is depicted wearing the uniform of a First Lieutenant, with two "pips" on the shoulder and carrying a sword. Asquith was killed on 15 September 1916 during the battle of the Somme. The connection of Raymond Asquith with the Manners family is very strong. He met Lady Constance Manners at her family home (Clovelly) in 1901 and was immediately won over as a friend and admirer – he describes her in a letter as "a really beautiful soul". Arthur Asquith, a younger brother of Raymond, was married to Betty Manners at All Saints on 30 April 1918. It is somewhat poignant to see the signatures of Lord Manners and Herbert Asquith on the wedding certificate – both their eldest sons had been killed in the war. New Zealand soldiers staying at Avon formed the guard of honour and gave a traditional Maori shout.

Lady Laura Lovat – the central Virgin Mary figure is Laura Lovat. She was Laura Lister before marriage. Her father, Lord Ribblesdale, married Charlotte Tennant. Charlotte's sister Margot was to be second wife of P.M. Asquith. Their father, Sir Charles Tennant, politician, art connoisseur and a trustee of the Royal Academy, was Scottish and so was Lord Lovat, a Catholic peer, who married Laura. Sir Charles's second son Frank commissioned Traquair in 1908 to decorate a newly designed grand piano for his home in Kent, Lympne Castle. Perhaps this brought her name to the fore when Lord Manners, whose family was becoming linked with Margot Asquith, Frank's sister, was looking for an artist for the mural in memory of Constance.

Lord William Cecil Bishop of Exeter – William was the father of Mary who later married Francis Lord Manners. William's love of poor people, and especially Romanies, was passed on to Mary – hence her interest in the settled travellers in the village.

Bishop Charles Gore of Oxford – one of the founders of Christian Socialism; Lord Tennyson – the poet; William Blake – the poet, much admired by Traquair and included in other works by her; Louis Pasteur - made many medical advances, especially bacteriology, a new science a hundred years ago; Lord Lister – very famous at the time and co-operated with Pasteur on similar research in England.

Postscript
All Saints has had its share of misfortune. Almost screened from view by Scots pine surrounding it, the gales of 1990 brought most of them down and local people took on the task of clearing up the mess. It is now replanted with ornamental trees and shrubs.

The lead was stolen from the roof in the 1950s and during repairs in 1998 the roof caught fire. It was saved by the quick action of the local fire brigade. The lead had been replaced by aluminium in the 1950s, which is now disintegrating. Water is getting in and damaging the mural. English Heritage have shown some interest in its restoration.

The Manners family still own large areas of land in the New Forest and continue to take an interest in All Saints. Lord Manners lives in Avon near Tyrrells Ford. Avon Tyrrell is an activity residential Leisure Centre, a charity in a family trust.

All Saints, Thorney Hill, is a very special place. Until the great storm of 1990 it was barely visible from the road. It looks more like a stately home than a church. It contains works by some world-renowned artists and craftsmen. And it is still "owned" by the traveller community – this is clear just by looking at the gravestones in the churchyard. As Canon Elkins has said:

"This building is not just a church or a collection of great art treasures. It depends for its genius on the people who commissioned it, their personalities, relationships (by turns, stormy, moving, romantic and outrageous) needs and emotions. This genius flows into the artists who created it, allowing their genius and innovation and creativity to bring such purposes to life. Thus All Saints is there for the Glory of God and commemorates Mary and John, brother and sister, two young people aged 17 and 21 cut down in their prime of life and appropriately two young artists of awe-inspiring genius – Blow and Gill - express glory and grief in their creations. Likewise Traquair and MacKennal bring the experience of maturity and reflection – at the very peak of their achievements. This building is a total expression and cannot be understood outside or disconnected from the human interactions recorded here. That is why it will remain a beautiful but sterile monument to the past until the characters come to life and begin to tell their story in these stones. Robert Lorimer, an architect and a close friend of Traquair, a man who gave her support and commissions (for example, the Frank Tennant piano) wrote in 1892 that her 'pictures are full of story, but not from the literary point of view.' Her work truly communicates without such devices. Perhaps the spirit of Ruskin was alive and well when his pupil Blow began this great work and others by their art brought it to perfection."

Blow, Gill, Traquair and MacKennal were not the only artists to be drawn to Thorney Hill. Amelia and Eliza Goddard, Sven and Juanita Berlin, Jenny Vize, Augustus John and Irene Soper were attracted by the culture and colour of the Gypsy community. Writers were similarly entranced, as can be seen in the vivid descriptions of Romany life by Alice Gillington, E. Stevens, Katherine Oldmeadow, Juliette de Bairacli Levy and Peter Tate.

3. Lighting Up

"Faded is the "Gold alight in the sky, And royal red in the heart of the heather"; twilight creeps up the bypaths between the brackens, and the nearing shadows of night keep step with a horde of way-spent travellers trudging heavily back to their tan. A flood of yellow light pouring forth from one of the tents shows a juvel, her brown face aglow in the light of a candle tied to a stick thrust in the ground, which a boy, kneeling dark against its radiance, has just set aflame with a brand from the fire. Its beacon-torch is leading home the lagging feet of that knot of wanderers, dimly discerned through the dusky trees, whose "wayfaring day is o'er," to

The House of the Open Door....
And all the night the stars go by,
Waving their silver swords together.

And the night hawk whistles softly over the darkened heath, and the bog-withy breath travels to and fro over the swiftly running streams."

The House of the Open Door is the title of an article by Alice Gillington about Amelia Goddard, which appeared in the *Journal of the Gypsy Lore Society* in 1908.

Amelia (1847-1928) and Eliza (1840-1915) Goddard were the daughters of Dr Goddard of Christchurch. They taught art at their studio in Bridge Street, Christchurch, but could not make a living at it, so after their parents' deaths they moved to Lark Gate at Thorney Hill. They gave a joint exhibition at the Dore Gallery, New Bond Street, London in 1904. Eliza liked to paint roses. Amelia was particularly interested in the Forest and the Gypsies who lived at Thorney Hill and quite often stayed amongst them in their camp. The Red House Museum at Christchurch has two of her paintings: a Gypsy girl's head, and a Gypsy encampment.

The House of the Open Door
"Beyond the grey Priory church, which has overlooked the twin rivers of the Stour and the Avon since the Doomsday book was written and the laws of the Red Forest King enacted, stands a tall white house, possibly of Georgian era, but in all probability much older in the rear part and out-buildings, whose windows open on to the wide water-meadows, the Creek, the Salmon-Run, and beyond all, the heather-capped ironstone headland that juts out into the open sea.

If you should enquire your way to this house – 'Tis the one with the green bushes about'n' say the townsfolk, 'close by Stony Lane'.

True! Without it has the green bushes about it, and the secrets of the woodlands are pictured within its walls. Outside a row of bushes along the railing bars it off from Purewell's narrow street.

Inside, the glamour of the forest surrounds one, with its scenes of misty dawns and rosy after-glows, golden noondays and dreamful gloamings over green lawns and heather-covered hills, gloomy woods and silver fords; its songs and legends, its past history and present-day romance – these two being merged in one.

For three generations has this house in Purewell been the dwelling-place of the Gypsy's Friend, each of whom were members, in his or her turn, of the oldest living family in the Priory town. To find the story of the first friendship, one must go back to a dark night over a hundred years ago, when the grandfather of the present generation was summoned in haste to the bedside of a Gypsy woman lying dangerously ill in the depths of the Forest. The Gypsy who had ridden over to fetch him, and who doubtless had good reasons of his own for concealing the way to the camp, having blindfolded the doctor, laid hold of his horse's bridle and led him through the wild recesses of the woods to the tent where the woman lay. But from that time forward he gained the firm and fast friendship of the Romany folk, after trusting himself fearlessly in their hands in the midst of the lonely Forest in the dark watches of the night.

Secondly, his son, following his father's profession, followed also in his footsteps forest-ward – he in his turn becoming known as the Gypsy's Friend.

Lastly, the two daughters, whom at his death he left to live on in this same tall, white, three-storied house, with its thick-hedged, high-walled, old-fashioned garden, its many rooms, spacious entrances, and long passages, its dark oak floors and panelled wainscots, blue willow-patterned china, red damask curtains and oaken settles, became by calling and inheritance the Gypsy's Friend.

Particularly is this title applicable to the Gypsy painter (the elder sister being a flower-painter), who has earned her living by her brush from her childhood up. And she dates her first attraction to the Gypsy race in general from the time when, a young student in Paris, she came across a Romany model in the studio of her master, M. Chapelin, who was descended, according to his own belief and his tribe's tradition, from Ishmael the son of Hagar.

To this day there is a hearty welcome in her house for the way-faring stranger and all who take the road. And the name of the Lady Goddards, as our Hampshire Gypsies designate them, is a passport into the hearts of some of the most distrustful, the surliest and wildest, as well as the most charming, of our south country travellers. Moreover, be it said, their name has saved many an unpleasant situation, when the novice to Romany ways and manners has made her debut on the stage of camp life. For instance, that August afternoon on Sholing Heath, when you fled from an infuriated *dai*, mad with drink and jealousy and hatred of the Gorgio, across the common, and Betsy Page's mother dragged you by the hand into her own caravan.

Or again, that winter's evening when you had to wait till long after nightfall in a strange camp, along with the ancient crone who travels in a dwarfish green caravan and is believed by the other Gypsies to be very wicked, waiting to see Lovinya, who was 'took bad with the Viper's Dance'; and Vanlo Bower's young wife, wonderfully picturesque in her yellow head-kerchief, her rosy coral beads, her striped silk *diklos,* came in to help you, and afterwards led you up the dark road homeward.

For their Lady Goddard has painted all the forest-born Gypsies, their *chavis, grais* and *vardos,* and they take delight in the part they played in the making of the picture.

Chuckled the old flower-seller over her basket of 'beowtiful daffs' or 'bit o'laycock' as she jogged along the road in her short ragged gown, up to her knee-high boots, with a battered hat on her head and a frowsy pipe in her mouth: 'She be one o' we, my dear! The Lady Goddard have a-lived in the Forest along o' we! Take a bunch o' bulrushes, my dear, and help a poor old doomun. She've a-tented along o' we, she have!" *Tatchipen si,* she has lived the Forest life in the tents of the Forest people, and here has portrayed all the everyday incidents of Gypsy life.

So let yourself be led by Gypsy hands, blindfolded though you may chance to be by Giorgio misgivings and prejudices, through the Forest by day and night, and 'you shall see what you shall see'.

But that was in the old days, before the great colony of Gypsy flower sellers with their tents had given way to the brick-kilns down in Gypsy Hollow, and the red brick house had made an ugly blot here and there among the squatters' cobwalls and thatched roofs. Bitterly do some of the older Gypsies regret that they were fools enough to sell the very ground under their feet – at a high value – to the insatiable brick-making and house-building Gorgio; and they would regain their lost footing if they could.

Meantime, the brown roof and the yellow walls of some of these squatters' cottages shelter many a Gypsy family, and the old Forest ballads are still sung, to the carousal of cakes and ale, as they gather round the wide hearth or group themselves against the summer twilight of open door and diamond pane. Still the Seven Firs on Thorney Hill stand as landmarks from the Forest to Wimborne and from Wimborne to Salisbury, and beckon to the ships passing up and down channel. Still the magpies flash from tree to tree above Gypsy Hollow.

Yet 'the tall white house with the green bushes about it,' down Purewell Street, knows the sisters no longer; for the Forest has taken back its own. And to the cottage at Lark's Gate, close to where the Seven Firs keep watch on Thorney Hill, Gypsy-painter and flower-painter, a-wearied with the increasing struggle for existence and the world's rush and unrest, have followed the *paterans* themselves into the wild, sweet heart of the Forest, to find a halting-place on life's hard journey in the ling, a shelter in the hollies, a light at eventide and a hearty welcome in the hearts of their Gypsy friends. And here the two painters work and wait, till for them, too,

The wayfaring day is o'er;
Thou and I, together we lie
In the House of the Open Door;
But for you and for me…
Wandering folk and poor,
There are dreams of delight on meadow and moor,
When the wind blows wild !"

Betty Gillington was the author of *Gypsies of the heath by the Romany Rawny* (1916). More details about the life of the Goddard sisters were given by their great great nephew, Tim Goddard, in *A Painter of Gypsies* (1998):

A Painter of Gypsies
"Amelia and her siblings were artists who lived much of their lives in Christchurch, Hampshire. Her father and grandfather were doctors who were called out, from time

to time, to tend to the needs of Gypsies in the New Forest. She took a particular interest in the Gypsies and many of her paintings are of Gypsy scenes and portraits in the New Forest.

It is said that this attraction dates back to about 1873, a time when she was a young student in Paris. She came across a Romany model in the studio of her master, M Chapelin, who was descended, so it is told, from Ishmael, the son of Hagar

Her father had purchased a property, Lark's Gate, at Thorney Hill in the New Forest, and both Amelia and her sister, Eliza, used it as a painting retreat. They moved there permanently around the turn of the century. It is from this residence that Amelia came to know Gypsies well, indeed she lived amongst them for much of her later life. An article about her, written by Alice E Gillington, was published in the *Gypsy Lore Society Journal* of October 1908. She was a member of that Society in 1909, and of the *Romanitshels', Didakais' and Lore-Folk Gazette* in 1912.

Thorney Hill had for many years been one of the main Gypsy sites in the New Forest. Some still lived in camps in the traditional way, with tents and carts and the occasional vardo (wagon). Amelia captured these scenes and people in oils, which featured bright colours of red and yellow. Her works included *Mary Stanley* (said to be the grand daughter of a Gypsy Queen), *Gypsy* (which was given to Louisa, Marchioness of Waterford), *A Mapolitan, A Neapolitan* and *Strewing the Pateran*.

Amongst my favourites are *Gypsies Halting by the Ling*, depicting two gaily painted caravans and a cart in a semi-circle on Magpie Green, which is close to holly-shelters near Thorney Hill, and *Lighting Up Time (The Candle in the Ground)*, with a flood of yellow light pouring from one of the tents and showing a juvel (woman) with her face aglow in the light of a candle tied to a stick thrust in the ground, which a boy, kneeling, has just set alight with a brand from the fire. Both of these paintings, with many others, were exhibited at the Dore Gallery in London in 1904, under the title, *The Knot of Grass*.

When she painted Gypsies, she had to pay them and times were hard. Her sole source of income appeared to be from selling her works and she promoted these by sending photographs of her paintings to many people. There is a record of her sending photographs of *The Pateran* to Dr D F de L'Hoste Ranking and *The Patrin* to Mr R A Scott MacFie, both officials of the Gypsy Lore Society."

E. Stevens
Living on the margin of society as they do, loving freedom and courting danger, the Gypsies also inspired an over-romanticised image of their way of life. Poets and novelists from Shakespeare to Sir Walter Scott used the vagrant Gypsy as a theme. Part of their treatment in later literature was due to George Borrow, whose books first brought the Gypsies to public notice. Borrow, who lived and travelled with the Romanies and who learned their various dialects, did care for more than just the picturesque in Gypsy life.

In terms of novels, the very little known *Allward* was written by the 17 year old daughter of the vicar at Burley, E. Stevens. Although a bit of a schmaltzy love story, contained within it is some of the most authentic writing about Gypsy life that you will ever read, set in and around Thorney Hill compound, Bransgore. How she ever got that close, in those times, is astonishing.

Juliette de Bairacli-Levy
Juliette de Bairacli Levy was a botanist and herbalist who lived and travelled in many lands. *Wanderers in the New Forest* (1958) tells of the three years she spent with her two young children in a primitive cottage in the Forest. To her keen and affectionate observation of ponies, birds, bees and plants is added a passionate plea for the ancient rights of the Gypsies with whom she claims kinship.

Juliette refers to "A Mrs Elizabeth Cooper, Gypsy, of Bromley, Kent" who "sent a well-written letter to the *News Chronicle*, protesting that in three successive cases of child-stealing recently, the Gypsies had been made suspect." This indicates that there might have been links between the Coopers of the New Forest and those in Bromley; by the same token, it is possible that there were connections between the Gypsy Patemans of Hampshire and those in Orpington.

Eliza Cooper was one of her longest-term friends amongst the New Forest Romanies. Juliette was told the story of how Eliza and her brother met a lady – "fair but strange-seeming" – who took them to a place in the Forest and told them to dig there. After they had dug around for a short while, a box was found containing some pieces of old money and jewellery:

"Eliza had her own experience of forest treasure. She related this to me with her usual childlike truthfulness and simplicity. Other Coopers far across the forest at Thorney Hill, spoke about Eliza's find to Jenny Vize: aged about seventy-five to eighty, they remembered it well."

Jenny Vize
Jenny Vize was an artist who mostly painted Gypsy life. When the Wessex biannual art exhibition was held, Jenny Vize entered two oil paintings of Gypsies, a family group, man, woman and child; and a van interior, with figures against the light of a fire-stove. Both pictures were accepted: and then came the deserved success. Jenny had used her Welsh origin name of Eryl Vize, and had written the Romany titles beneath the English ones:

"In the following Wessex biannual exhibition, Eryl Vize had three Gypsy pictures hung. I remember the excitement later when she took one of those pictures to show Gypsy friends gathered in *The Crown Inn* at Bransgore. She showed her pictures of Gypsies in a compound, and the always critical Gypsies were enthusiastic about the way the artist had put their people on to her canvas." (Levy)

Irene Soper
A painting of New Forest Gypsies by Eryl Viz can be found in *The Romany Way* (1994) by Irene Soper. In her chapter on the New Forest Gypsies, Irene talks about "my three hundred year old thatched cottage at Abbots Well near Fordingbridge, an original forester's cabin and one of the few left standing. In the past the cottage has been lived in by foresters, artists, writers and more recently by herbalist and friend of the Romanies, Juliette de Bairacli Levy."

Irene was visited by Eliza Cooper; "I think she liked to see again the cottage where she spent so much of her time with Juliette. Eliza, who admitted to being over eighty, still worked at the market garden where she lived in a caravan. Together with other local Gypsies, she hoed the weeds from between the rows of lettuce and strawberry plants." Irene was also visited by Eliza's grandson, Wally Cooper. Another visitor was Annie Cooper, also in her eighties, who walked into Fordingbridge and back each morning – a distance of three miles. She sold spring flowers and made holly wreaths and paper flowers.

Annie had two passions – one was her ponies and the other was collecting paintings. Irene painted Annie with her favourite gray mare called Feather. Annie also had a painting by Augustus John, given to her by one of John's sons. Today the Gypsies still deal in ponies which they run on the Forest. They also work on the land in the market gardens or the strawberry fields. Apart from the traditional items such as clothes pegs and paper flowers the forest Gypsies also made ash casks for the foresters' mead.

November the 26th is the traditional date on which the Gypsies are allowed to start picking holly to sell at the markets and to make wreaths. At one time they filled their sacks with moss gathered from the boggy paths on the side of the hill above Abbots Well. This they used as the foundation of the wreaths. But it is no longer permissible to pull moss or any other plant.

Augustus John
Fordingbridge will always remain associated with the New Forest Gypsies for it was here that their champion and friend Augustus John lived. The famous painter, known to the Gypsies as Sir Gustus, was looked upon by many of them as their King. As President of the Gypsy Lore Society he fought very hard for these people to retain their rights to travel and settle where they liked in the forest. However, bureaucracy ensured that these ancient rights would not continue despite other traditional uses, such as hunting, that were allowed to continue.

Katherine Oldmeadow
Juliette de Bairacli-Levy's other interest was herbs and she was the author of *The Illustrated Herbal Handbook*. Juliette's passion for Gypsies and herbs was shared by Katherine Louise Oldmeadow (1878-1963), who lived in Highcliffe, near Christchurch, on the borders of the New Forest. Miss Oldmeadow wrote a series of children's books, from *Princess Anne* (1925) to *Three Corners Camp* (1958). She was equally at home in the drawing room at Highcliffe Castle, where she would visit Violet Stuart Wortley CBE, or in a Gypsy's shack at Thorney Hill, where she would mix with the Gypsies collecting information. They helped her with *The Folklore of Herbs* (1946).

Levy describes an "exciting art event in the New Forest which turned into a Gypsy gathering, when there was a joint exhibition of the paintings of Sven and Juanita Berlin at the Bladon Gallery near Andover, with Augustus John opening the exhibition. Sven's pictures were mostly of the New Forest Gypsies, and they came in a group to see themselves in the paintings: Juanita's work was primarily horses and other animals."

Juanita Berlin

"Juanita, a very Gypsy-like figure, with her long black hair falling over her orange coat, with her ear-rings made from short strings of Victorian farthings glinting through the hair; horse brasses for her jewellery with further a coral necklace from which hung a strange, old coin thought to be of ancient Russian origin, the approximate size of the former English five-shilling piece, but dug up in the New Forest by a Gypsy, and presented to Juanita by the finder. Yet despite the flamboyant clothes, which I admired, the artist's personality was quiet and shy." (Levy)

"Juanita, whom I called Ishtar, had become my second wife as soon as I was free to remarry…She claimed to be a Gypsy and looked like one: even the Gypsies thought that. I don't know if she was a Gypsy: I never thought so. What made it difficult to tell was that she had been educated at a school in Lymington and spoke like a lady most of the time, but changed her voice when she was with Gypsies or swore appallingly when she chose. She dressed like a Gypsy and had long Prussion Blue hair like an Indian woman. I called her Ishtar because she was like the Cretan goddess of that name whom she much admired." (Berlin).

Juanita lived in a Gypsy wagon with Sven Berlin at Shave Green in the New Forest between 1953-55. She wrote about the families which they lived with and came to know very well in *The Gypsies of the New Forest* (1960):

"There are still well-known Gypsy families living in the Forest, which have been mentioned by many famous writers, families long associated with the Forest. John R. Wise, writing on the Forest Gypsies in 1863, mentions the Stanleys, Lees, Burtons and Snells. Today there are Smiths, Greens, Stanleys, Boswells, Wells, Sherrards, Lees, Peters, Lovells, Jameses, Coopers, Kings, Barneys, one Lock (a nephew of the celebrated Esmerelda), the Hughes (associated with the Dorset branch of this name) and the occasional visit from other counties of Brazils and Woods.

These days the New Forest Gypsy lives either in a house (which nevertheless shows its Gypsy occupancy by countless signs), or in one of the four camps or compounds which were opened in 1927 or thereabouts, for the only reason 'officialdom' couldn't keep track of them…to the question 'Where are the Gypsies?' the answer is 'Gone'."

Juanita also wrote about her experiences at Shave Green in *Life with Sven – The Wagon Years* (Casey):

"We stayed for two years camped in the Forest where Sven began to paint the Gypsies, our first visitors, who had somehow known of our coming and who became our friends. When we had to move, we found a field to rent nearby and put up a shed as well. Here Sven painted with more freedom, resting every afternoon when a bantam regularly laid an egg on his chest while he dozed!

Gradually, we began to make some money, wheeling and dealing, 'totting' with the Gypsies and like them dressing ourselves in other people's cast-offs. Sometimes Victorian dresses or a London gentleman's tweed overcoat. Jasper played with toys scavenged off rubbish dumps, brought to him by doting travellers. We drank with them, danced with them, went to the Derby with them on the back of a lorry and mourned with them.

Without avarice and without envy, they lived for the day, the hour; time was the passing of the seasons, not the consulting of clocks. They transcended the muddy 'compounds' where they were incarcerated by officialdom. No water, no electricity, no floors allowed. We shared their penury, their hopes and their occasional good luck."

Sven Berlin

"There was the big figure of the dark Sven, in a dark felt wide-brimmed hat, gamekeeper-like clothes of beech mast brown corduroy jacket and trousers, high leather boots; a warm and friendly personality" (Levy).

A major exhibition of Sven Berlin's paintings was held at the St Barbe Museum and Art Gallery, Lymington, in 2003. Steve Marshall, curator at the museum, wrote an introduction to the exhibition catalogue, *Gold in the Dust – the Gypsy paintings of Sven Berlin* (2003):

"It is exactly fifty years since Sven Berlin journeyed from St Ives to the New Forest in a Gypsy caravan. Over the next ten years or so he was to produce an immensely powerful body of work focussing on the New Forest Gypsies. Berlin has always principally been known as a sculptor, and indeed he himself viewed flat canvas or paper as a great limitation when compared to the three dimensions of sculpture. Yet he felt that, in the case of the Gypsy paintings, oils provided the perfect medium to capture the natural colour of his subjects and to contrast it with the shadowy, aqueous light of the forest.

Sven Berlin (1911-1999) was a colourful and bohemian character who had been a leading figure in the post-war art scene at St Ives. Disenchanted with life in Cornwall, Berlin and his wife Juanita went in search of the Forest Gypsies with whom they were to develop a remarkably close relationship. The Gypsies had been barred from camping in the open Forest back in the 1920's and were given the choice of living in one of six Compounds or in Council Housing. Conditions at the camps could be atrocious, most had no running water and the inhabitants were banned from building any kind of a permanent structure and lived in caravans or tents.

Yet amongst such sadness Berlin was to find the inspiration for one of the most intensely creative periods of his career. His pictures represent an honest and at times heart-rending record of a people trying to retain their dignity in the face of overwhelming odds. Few people have ever been accepted by the Romany people in quite the same way as Sven Berlin, and it is a tribute to his integrity as a man and as an artist that he was allowed such freedom to record the Gypsies' last days among the trees of the New Forest."

Dromengro

Sven wrote about his experiences at Shave Green in *Dromengro* (1971), a fiercely poetic and haunting book in which he tells of his quest for the Gypsy people; the real Gypsy that still existed, half hidden by the tapestries and poems that had been woven around him, "dragging with him the magic of Ur, the gold of Syria, his music and dancing and skills with horses." With his close friend Augustus John he sought the reality behind the legend and found that reality and legend were one:

"Dromengro is the Gypsy word for Man of the Road. I was never a Gypsy, nor have wanted to be, but they are a race of people whom destiny drew me near and whom I lived with and grew to love. In this way I became a Man of the Roads, much as Borrow was known as Lavengro, Man of the Words, though only like to that great writer on Gypsies in this one respect, for he was afraid of love and sometimes tendentious."

Berlin's interest in Gypsies was awakened by his aunt Dickie Slade, who used to tell him stories of living with the Gypsies in Rye and Romney Marsh in Kent: "They lived in wagons with hordes of children and dressed like Gypsies some of the time; though I don't think there was much travelling done or that they were any good handling horses and had to rough it."

Berlin had also glimpsed Gypsies on fairgrounds and racecourses: "I had seen an Old Woman, Gypsy Lee – *Purrum*, they called her – dressed in long black Victorian skirts and a huge hat with ostrich feathers of orange and violet *dukkerin*, which is telling fortunes, from the steps of her wagon outside Bromley fair". This is probably a reference to the Uraniah Boswell of Farnborough, Kent, which is where many of my Gypsy Patemans were born and lived. Berlin had also seen Gypsies at Mitcham Fair, and I have records of Gypsy Patemans living on Mitcham Common.

Sven describes his first encounter with the Gypsies of the New Forest: "I (stepped) into the trees where the Gypsies had gone. This was the first time I had been under the trees in the sense of a moving creature in nature. I was spellbound by the underneath light that was both kinetic and aqueous, as though one were under the water, and the great shapes of shadow and reflected light moving silently like fish. The tall trees were like sentinels in a green city under the sea. This was the magic of the Forest that could beguile a man to his death. But instead of meeting Undine of the waters or hearing the singing of Sirens I heard the harsh barking of dogs and the voices of children as I broke into an open area of uneven ground with high mounds and pits and tall beech trees, which cast over everything the same green light. Each at a different level were the tents and huts of several families of Gypsies."

Berlin witnessed the end of traditional Gypsy life in the New Forest: the Gypsies' camping-grounds closed, their people forced into Council houses, crushed by a society which cannot tolerate the exceptional, the eccentric or the nomadic. No more would it be possible for Borrow's Petulengro to say: "There's night and day, brother, both sweet things; sun, moon, and stars, brother, all sweet things; there's likewise a wind on the heath. Life is very sweet brother…" For the Gypsy, the wind on the heath no longer blows:

"One by one the old Gypsies died, mostly before they left the Compound. Old Jesse, Young Jesse, George Wells, Dosha, Priscilla, Millie, the Bechstein Bat. One of the young girls even hanged herself. It was sad beyond belief. Those who survived fared little better. As one of the old women said to me in the street: 'I lights a bit a *yog* in me garden and cooks the *scran* but it ain't the same as being up the woods. 'Ouse ain't no good to the likes a we. The old uns are dying like flies.'

Black Fred hung on for a time. I saw him once at Thorny Hill after they had closed the Compound there, searching for something or other he had left behind, and then again on the moor, when he turned and seemed to light his fag-end off one of the catalyst flames at Fawley, with all the ingenuity of a man who had lived on the hard edge of life for so long. He smiled with his paralysed face which was now half-hidden by a grey beard, and waved sadly. Soon after I heard that he too had died. Only the strawberry growers did well, buying their own plot and house."

The gifted New Forest bones player and step-dancer Ted 'Darkie' Duckett, lived for a large part of his life at Hangar Corner on the Beaulieu Road. He married the daughter of Bert Doe, who had served in the cavalry compound at Denney Lodge before the widespread rehousing of all New Forest Gypsies in the new housing estates built at Hythe, Thorney Hill and Totton after the Second World War.

A vibrant painting by Sven Berlin, *Gypsies Dancing* (1956) depicts both bone-playing and step-dancing and shows the colour and energy traditionally associated with Gypsies. Sven describes the event:

"…but out of the experience of dancing with them at Christmas in the Workmen's Club at Pilley and getting so drunk that Benny was hit over the head with a bottle in mistake for someone who was supposed to be carrying a bag of sovereigns; out of playing the bones and the spoons while the wild old men did extraordinary tap dances with fantastic vigour, as though animated separately by strings; out of the sudden laughter, or wailing from grief released in drink (for the Gypsies do not talk of their dead – they walk at their elbows); out of all this I made paintings with a new vitality from the source of things, involving once more the human drama with the mysteries of invention from the darkness of the mind. In the dust there was still gold."

Sven painted *Gypsy Mother and Child* in 1966. This dark and brooding Madonna and child has a timeless, ancient feel and is thought to be a portrait of Rosie Smith and her baby. Rosie and her family were among the last to leave Shave Green. Sven came across her again, years later, selling flowers in Lymington market, her beauty worn by a hard life. It is possible that this chance encounter (the last with any of the Shave Green Gypsies) inspired him to paint this poignant study – the final chapter in a tragedy:

"Often when I see Rosie selling flowers in the street, I think on these things and of how I made the journey from Trafalgar Square to Christchurch Priory as a boy, and on to discover Shave Green, and one day to find a large painted notice nailed to the pine trees after they had closed the Compound near Bransgore.

THE CITY OF THORNEY HILL

Is what it said, in large primitive letters that carried their own kind of dignity and pride."

Peter Tate
Peter Tate mentions Sven Berlin in his stories of *The New Forest 900 Years After* (1979): "Berlin tried once to go back to his well-loved Shave Green when the compound was in decline – not that it had ever been anything else as long as the gawjo held the reins and you needed a permit even to be there – only to find that he, who had been prala (brother) to the Coopers, the Wellses, the Lees and the Smiths

was now the gawjo, the outsider. He traced a few friends to Thorney Hill and to the cemetery."

Tate also visited the old compounds, looking for the grandchildren of Gypsies who once lived there: "They are not at Thorney Hill. The area where the local council erected prefabricated chalets to house the travellers, thinking that that might have been an improvement on their canvas or wheeled concoctions, was semi-cleared for a long time, with brambles thriving upon the concrete standings. Now, even the concrete is gone to make a car-free zone and the lawn is so authentic – the product of an alliance between the Forestry Commission and New Forest District Council – that it might always have been that way. Down the road towards Bransgore, several Council houses have a slightly wild look about them, as though their tenants would sooner be out than in. But these same people have already announced to the local authority that they are not Needies or Diddekoi or tinker or anything in between. They are householders, just like the rent book says. If you were looking for roots, they would lean over the chain-link fences which separate their gardens from the road and deny them."

4. Mary Stanley

"First and foremost stands Mary Stanley, the granddaughter of the Gypsy queen, with the dark forest for a background, framed in the very oak that once formed part of the Miraculous Beam in the Priory roof." Mary Stanley, *"Queen of the Gypsies"*, was buried in 1797 in the churchyard of St Andrew at Landford.

In his book *The Rural Life of England* (1844) William Howitt notes that "The New Forest has long been a great haunt of Gypsies, particularly of one remarkable family – the Stanleys". Howitt then gives more information about the Stanleys, based on information supplied by Mrs Southey:

"The Gypsies who mostly frequent this neighbourhood - or did frequent it, for their visits are now 'few and far between' – are Lees and Stanleys. Some years ago a party of these Stanleys came from a distant part of the country to attend a wedding at Newport, in the Isle of Wight. They stopped at the turnpike-gate near my house, being on friendly terms with the toll man and his family, who had often done them kind offices, and to the daughter who is now in my service (1838) they entrusted the important office of making up grey silk spencers and smart flowered chintz petticoats for each of the women; encamping in the neighbourhood while the work was in hand, and 'very particular' the ladies were about 'good fits' etc. Then they went to the best hatters in the town, and ordered hats on purpose for them – of the long felt, wide brimmed sort for the women. The tradesmen hesitated giving credit, as they required, till their return from the island, at which they were highly indignant. 'What!' stormed one, whom they called Brother John –'What! Refuse credit to a gentleman rat catcher!' But they obtained it, and paid honourably on their return, and as honestly remunerated the seamstress.

This same party often encamped at a spot in the Forest called Marlpit Oak – and nearer to my residence on a hill near the road, called Gally Hill, and were not ill thought of by the farmers and poor people, and one or two forest girls would sometimes steal to their tents, sure of a savoury regale. The wonder is how they lived so well – for their kettles were not filled with the produce of poaching, or of thefts in the hen roost – still less with meat 'that had died of its own accord', as the people say. No; they used frequently to go back from the town laden with good joints honestly purchased and paid for at the butcher's.

On one occasion, a day or two before Easter Sunday, Brother John and two of the ladies of the tribe displayed their marketing to my neighbours at the turnpike gate – a fine breast, loin, and leg of veal. 'Tomorrow's Easter Sunday', said they, 'and we always have a feast of veal on that day.' 'How can you contrive to roast it at your fires?' inquired the woman who was now my servant. 'Better a deal than you can at your poor pinched in grates' was the answer; 'and then we shall have rice puddings.' 'But you can't bake, if you can roast?' 'Can't we? Come and taste if you ever knowed better baking in your life.' And then they described their culinary process. Having mixed their ingredients – all of the best – in a large brown pan of that sort of ware which is fireproof, they covered it with another of the same sort, set it deep in a bed of glowing peat ashes, and heaped it over to a foot depth with the same.

There were seven daughters of this particular family of the Stanleys, all splendid beauties; - one but too celebrated, 'the beautiful Caroline Stanley'. She fell into worse company than that of her own people, and on two or three occasions was absent from them for a year and more at a time, living in splendour as 'maitresse en titre', to more than one officer of high rank; dashed about in elegant carriages, clothed in 'silken sheen', and all sorts of bravery, and carried it with a high hand through her seasons of 'bad eminence.' But all the while she was out of her element; the free creature of the woods pined to be there again; and some fine morning she would be off without leave taking, and leaving behind her every atom of the dear bought finery that had become fetters to her. I knew her well by sight, and such a Cleopatra of regal beauty I never could have imagined to myself.

A short time before her first initiation in civilisation and corruption, I saw her showing off in high style. I called to give some order to my milliner, but sat quietly down to wait her leisure, finding her engaged in high disputation with the Gypsy beauty, who was rating her in no measured terms for some deviation from orders in the making of a bonnet which Caroline was in the act of trying on before the glass. And such airs and graces she gave herself! I never was more diverted.

'Woman!' she called the poor milliner, at every sentence. 'Did you think, because I'm a Gypsy, I'd wear such a thing as this,' said she, and dashed off the bonnet – an expensive one of black velvet, with a deep lace flounce – to the farther end of the room. When I last heard of her, a few years back, she was wandering – withered and haggard – with her diminished tribe. It has been much diminished of late years by the conviction and transportation of many of the men for horse stealing; of their proficiency in which I have had sad experience. Some years ago, I lost a very beautiful and favourite pony, at the same time that a rather valuable mare was stolen from a neighbour of mine (a farrier), and a young Galloway from another man, named Edward Pierce. Having done everything in our power to regain our lost steeds, we at last gave up the pursuit as useless.

Nearly two years afterwards, my neighbour, the farrier, came to ask me if I would join him and Pierce in some further endeavours to recover the stolen horses, which we had a fair chance of doing, he thought, according to the letter he presented for my perusal, a curious one it was, dated, 'The Hulks, Portsmouth'. The writer (one of the Stanleys) stated, that having been condemned to seven years' transportation, for a recent offence, he wished to stock himself with a few comforts for his voyage, and therefore, if we, the losers of such and such horses, stolen at such a time, would make it 'worth his while', he would put us in a way to have them back again. He began his letter (it was addressed to Pierce), 'Dear friend', and said at the conclusion, that not liking to go by his own name in such a place, and in his present circumstances, he had taken the liberty to use his, and begged to be addressed as Edward Pierce.

One of the girls Stanley married a Blake, and prosperous vagabonds they were – kept a chaise-cart, and a fine horse, with expensive plated harness. On the occasion of the christening of their first child, which took place at Beaulieu, they invited all the farmers and respectable country folk for miles round to a feast on the heath, and a sumptuous feast it was, and every thing 'done decently and in order'. Abundance of good things, eatables and drinkables. The tables, borrowed for the occasion, almost elegantly spread. Liquor in abundance, good ale and strong, but no abuse of it.

Fiddling and dancing afterwards till the long summer day closed in, and then the wild hosts and their civilised guests parted with mutual good will; the most respectable of the latter (good substantial farmers, their wives and families) protesting they had never been so well treated, or in company more decently conducted."

As a nomadic people the Gypsies were food gatherers and hunters of small game; they were also experts in animal lore and herbal medicine. So the forests and woodlands of England were favoured places to the Gypsies and Hampshire's New Forest, with its abundance of herbs and other medicinal plants, its wild game and fresh springs of water, was for many centuries a well-loved Gypsy haunt.

The first Gypsy immigrants probably crossed the English Channel and arrived in the southern Home Counties of Kent, Sussex and Hampshire. The New Forest Gypsies could have been some of the earliest settlements, before the Gypsies spread out across the country. The setting was ideal – a vast woodland, close to local towns for trade, and friendly local people. The enclosure of land may have driven more Gypsies into the Forest, as well as some local folk, which lead to some mixed relationships and marriages.

There is a reference to Gypsies in the New Forest in the Southampton Stewards book of 1555/56. The Gypsies and the local people came to rely on each other and co-existed quite happily. The Gypsies produced goods and crafts to trade and helped to locate lost and stranded livestock. Down the timeline Gypsies show a record of mixed fortunes, from being a Royal Mistress – Winifred Wells, mistress to Charles II – to being falsely accused and hanged for the murder of a Doctor – as in a case at Wellow in the nineteenth century. Later exoneration from that crime did little to help the executed man of course. Even a village on the edge of the Forest was founded by a Gypsy – a Willet was the first to build a clodden hut, (turves built in layers like bricks into a sort of beehive shape) at a place we now know as Nomansland.

There is a reference to Gypsies in Gilbert White's *The Natural History of Selborne* (1775) which mentions the Stanley family. In addition to the Stanleys there were several other well established families. Many of these were still around in 1899 when Rose C. de Crespigny and Horace Hutchinson wrote *The New Forest Its Traditions, Inhabitants and Customs*:

"Altogether there are about seventy families of Gypsies in the Forest. At present the principal names among them are Ayres, Coopers, Does, Greens, Sherreds, Lakeys, Williams, Peters, Stanleys, Wells, Whites, James, Burtons and Hughes. The Stanleys were the 'royal' family in olden times, and later the kingship passed to the Lees, a very old Gypsy family. The Lees are now all but extinct, having for their sole representative an old woman whose present name is Pidgely. With her the old kingly line will come to an end. She keeps the name Lee on her van, but so far as one can discover lays no claim to the title of 'queen.' At least it is never accorded her; and, indeed, the monarchical idea seems to have died out amongst them, for there is no acknowledged king or queen of the Gypsies today."

The Condition of the Gipsies
A Summary Account of the Proceedings of a Provisional Committee associated at Southampton with a view to the consideration and improvement of the Condition of

the Gipsies was published in 1828. This committee was established after "the trial of William Proudly, a Gipsey, for horse stealing; of which the result was the condemnation and execution of the unhappy man. His wife, an interesting young person of twenty-two years of age, was in the outer court, with an infant in arms. Patience Proudly (the widow), having been persuaded to abandon the roving and irregular habits of her former associates, was settled, together with a Gypsy lad of eleven years of age, by name Job Stanley, in a house in Southampton, on which they entered on 29 August 1827.

Shortly afterwards, an elderly family, Rose Proudly, aunt of Patience; and another family, consisting of a woman (Sally Hicks) and three children who had been forsaken of their father followed the example. The children were placed at an Infant School, and a small allowance was made to the retrospective parents for their board; the women receiving only occasionally a trifling pecuniary assistance, in addition to the rent of the house.

The children have made fair advancement at the infant school. One of these children (a lad of the age of twelve) has been placed with a carpenter; and a boy, by name Henry Stanley, six years old, was voluntarily given up by his mother to be boarded and educated at the Kingsland Infant School. These children seem much attached to their master (with some exception in the case of Job Stanley).

Patience Proudly is a monument of Divine grace in the conversion of the heart to the fear and love of God. The remarks of the elder of the other two women, Rose Proudly, were gratifying: she too seemed thankful for the kind interest shown for herself and the ignorant people with whom she had associated for fifty years. Of the third female, Sally Hicks, the sub-committee cannot speak so favourably. She had lately heard of the death of an only brother in a fight, on occasion of a quarrel at the public house, which had very deeply affected her.

Charlotte Stanley, well known in the county by the appellation of 'The Handsome Gipsey' (wife of a man now in the hulks) with four sons having expressed a desire to settle, a house has been provided for her. Maria Stanley, mother of Charlotte, is now residing with her daughter and is learning to read. Two of the boys, of fourteen and thirteen years of age have been taken on to the employ of Mr Jones, coach-maker, of Southampton; the two youngest are placed at an Infant School.

Lucy Stanley, an aged Gypsy, now residing at Southampton has been a Christian for thirty five years; and, not long after her own conversion, was made the honourable instrument of bringing her brother, William Stanley, to acknowledge the truth."

In 1891 the Association for the Improvement of the Breed of the New Forest Ponies was founded, principally to improve the quality of stallions in the Forest. They also organised stallion shows and races on Balmer Lawn. The races stopped during the Great War, but the shows went on, and convalescent Belgian soldiers got drunk at the 1917 show. Many years later, the Red Cross ladies, trying to cope with Thorney Hill Gypsies who had over indulged and started fighting, were impressed by the local Doctor's treatment – he threw a bucket of water over them! The races and shows were stopped again during World War Two. The first post war show drew a record entry and a record gate. A grey race pony bought from the Thorney Hill Gypsies won the ridden class.

An Old Woman's Outlook in a Hampshire Village
Charlotte Young's *An Old Woman's Outlook in a Hampshire Village* was published in 1892: "One genuine family was here some years ago, of thoroughly Gypsy blood. A woman was very ill, and a kind gentleman let them remain in his field and sent broth and wine. They were strictly honest, and even refused offers of help from other quarters, saying that they were fully provided for. The woman died, and they lamented her with loud cries like Easterns. They talked of putting a stone up to her, but have never done so. Her name was Gerania.

Rev. Stephen Butler went among the Gypsies on Soberton Downs. There was a regular camp there and a family named Stanley did attend the Soberton Anglican Church. Rev. Stephen Butler did christen quite a few of the Gypsy children and one of the Stanley girls was named after one of the Butler girls. Her name was Maryanne Butler."

A report was published in the journal of the Hampshire Field Club of 1893 concerning "The Gypsies of the New Forest" by R.W.S. Griffith. The number of Gypsies living in the Forest was estimated at "about 60 families numbering 400 men, women and children". Their regular camping grounds included Crock Hill, Ipley, Thorney Hill, Bransgore and Bartley. They lived "among holly bushes or thick undergrowth" and their names included Stanley, Lee, Eyre, Cooper and Burton.

"They are makers of tin ware, tinkers, umbrella menders, chair bottomers, clothes peg makers, beehive and basket makers, chimney sweeps, rag and bone collectors, etc. At Christmas time the men are busy making skewers and clothes pegs, in the summer they make bee-hives of grass or straw, and very good basket work." They also sell wild flowers and make artificial flowers.

The report contains photographs of Hannah Lakey "Queen of the Gypsies" and the Rose family, who were living at Hilltop, Beaulieu in 1893. "Comparatively well dressed, owning a cart, and therefore of a slightly higher position – decent respectable people, who move about considerably."

"In summer and harvesting time they move away to the harvest and hopping grounds, and earn some ready money by pea picking, hay making, harvesting and hop picking, the farmers in many instances preferring Gypsy to casual village labour, for the Gypsy is most reliable, generally an excellent workman, and invariably very civil."

Many Gypsy baptisms and weddings took place at hopping time and several Patemans were baptised at Binstead and Holybourne during the hop harvest.

"Mrs Lakey, considered the last 'Queen' of the New Forest Gypsies, died at the age of 85 in October 1903. She spent the first 80 years of her life in a tent in robust health and apparent happiness. But during 1898 she was very ill and encouraged to go into a cottage at Beaulieu Rails, a little hamlet of cottages about 1 mile to the west of Beaulieu village, where she lived in peace and quiet for the last five years of her life."

It is generally believed that there was spontaneous outcry against Gypsies by residents of the Forest. But in all his dealings with the true Foresters over a period of more than 50 years, Vesey-Fitzgerald never found any deep-seated hostility. The trouble began, he reasoned, in the years after World War 1 when the "newly-wealthy townsfolk, jealous of their status", began moving in and worrying about "the tone of the place".

The Gypsies were described as a "nuisance" and a "difficulty" in a 1913 report of the *House of Commons Select Committee on Commons (Inclosure and Regulation)*. Mr Perkins (a local MP) asked whether the Gypsies had caused any problems and Lord Arthur Cecil (a comparatively recent resident) replied: "They are a great nuisance to everybody. We hold that the Crown there are wrong. They will not help us, and will not allow us to shift the Gypsies. I am specially troubled by Gypsies myself. I have two instances which I cannot turn them away from within 100 yards of my house."

In 1926 the Forestry Commission created seven compounds for the Gypsies where they could stay without a time restriction. The seven original compounds were Blackhamsley, Broomhill, Hardley, Latchmoor, Longdown, Shave Wood, Thorney Hill. Later these were Broomhills, Ipley, Shave Green, Thorney Hill, Blackhamsley, Gritnam, Hardley. These compounds had no water or sanitation and it was a big change in lifestyle to be herded into a compound but in time these became dynamic communities in their own right.

Chief Traveller's Death
Christchurch Times, Saturday 5 March, 1927: "The funeral took place on Monday of the late Mr Noah Hughes, who was also known as 'Sandy Cooper', and who passed away at 4 Pound Lane, Christchurch, on the preceding Thursday at the age of 75 years. The deceased was widely known over the three counties of Hampshire, Dorset and Wiltshire, which he travelled in a caravan for nearly seventy years, and he was known by the fraternity of caravan dwellers as the 'Chief Traveller', the occupation of these people being that of licensed hawkers.

Word was quickly spread of his passing, and during the week-end scores of the fraternity visited Pound Lane to view the body and to pay their last respects to their departed 'chief', who, we are informed, is succeeded by his brother, Mr Sam Hughes, of Bristol. The deceased, who is stated to have been born on the Town Common, had 15 children – nine of whom are living – and three of them presented him with 36 grand-children, one with 14 and two others with 11 each.

There were a great number of mourners at the funeral, each of them carrying a wreath, many of which were of a most beautiful nature. The officiating clergyman was the Rev. A.B. Bennett, and the undertaking arrangements were in the hands of Miller Bros."

On 12 February 1932 "Mrs Lavinia Bowers died aged 75 and in accordance with her last wishes the Gypsies of Botany Bay, Sholing, Southampton burned her caravan and possessions on the common at Botany Bay. Except when she was on the road she spent all her days at Botany Bay. Her family established the Gypsy colony there 100 years ago. Widow of Noah Bowers, known as Chalky and since he died almost 20 years ago, she had been regarded as head of the colony."

Permits to use the compounds (and nowhere else) were issued to each family. These permits were attached to thirteen conditions, as spelt out in a report of the New Forest Association in 1938: "There are seven compounds at Blackhamsley, Broomhill, Hardley, Latchmoor, Longdown, Shave Wood, Thorney Hill. The illustrations are from photographs taken at Thorney Hill, an area with many holly trees....The number in the family have to be stated on the form and the conditions are as follows: 1. Dwellers in the encampment will at all times behave in a quiet and seemly manner…13. Should this permit be withdrawn for any reason the holder will be liable to exclusion from camping anywhere in the Forest."

In time the compounds were largely only used for winter quarters. The system was tightened up during the Second World War, when all the Gypsies were put into five compounds and not allowed to move between them. The demand for scrap metal led to the development of this Gypsy trade. The Thorney Hill compound was very large but Shave Green was the best known. In 1946 a committee was set up to look at the condition of the New Forest, including the compounds. The committee report (1947) claimed:

"While the standard of people throughout the country is steadily being raised, a group is allowed to live in the Forest which has hardly reached the standard of the Stone Age. The Gypsies, it is true, have not been heard in their own defence, but we have visited their camps and we should hesitate to describe them in detail. Even the picturesque element which appeals to the imagination of their defenders is here entirely lacking. Whatever may have been the case in earlier times, those of today show little of the true Romany strain and a very few only maintain the old Romany way of life with its comparatively high standards. The simple solution is to remove the Gypsies as soon as possible to some place at least five miles distant from the perambulations of the Forest…the Forest compounds can no longer be tolerated.

According to a census taken in early 1942, the camps and inhabitants are as follows: Broomhills 44 persons, Ipley 49, Shave Green 131, Thorney Hill 161, Black Hamsley 46, Gritnam 20. Total 451. All the camps with the exception of Thorney Hill are outside the limits of supply of a Statutory Water Undertaking. We suggest that camps should be established where services can be supplied. The selection of the site would present some difficulty. All concerned are anxious to remove these blots from the open waste of the New Forest. We would regard the Gypsies as persons of the working classes. They would graduate to Council houses and become the Council's tenants in the ordinary way."

A momentum now developed to close the compounds and house the Gypsies. This shaped the government policy on Gypsies in the 1960s. A survey in 1959 indicated that there were nearly one thousand Gypsies in Hampshire and that just under half of these were living in New Forest compounds. By 1960 the New Forest Rural District Council and the Ringwood and Fordingbridge Rural District Council began to move local Gypsies into ex-military camps (such as the disused huts of former Air Force bases at Ibsley and Holmsley, near Thorney Hill) and then into houses.

It is difficult for the house-dweller to appreciate the tremendous adjustments the Gypsy has to make in this transition to a settled life, and no provision was made for his traumatic experience until intermediate camps were established. The Hampshire

County Council set up four of these special camps: at North Baddesley, at Headley Down near Bordon, at Yateley and at Thorney Hill near Christchurch. Each camp had a warden and a training officer.

The Gypsies lived in pre-fabricated bungalows and attended classes to learn how to use electricity, how to cook and sew and generally keep house. Some also learned to read and write. Many of the men dealt in scrap metal, a direct development from their earlier tradition of horse dealing, but this was discouraged in favour of regular employment. By July 1966 nearly all the men living in three of Hampshire's special housing centres were working as general labourers on building sites, as lorry drivers or park attendants. Advantage was taken of the Hampshire Gypsy's special knowledge of the Forest and many of the less shrewd "horse and cart" men were employed in forestry work.

About one hundred families were settled in council houses from Hampshire's intermediate camps, and the programme was so successful that the North Baddesley and Headley Down camps were closed. This was not achieved without difficulty, however, for the Gypsies had strong feeling of identity and many Hampshire Gypsies who accepted wage-earning jobs and permanent housing are said to have lost prestige among the rest of their self-employed travelling race.

Of course, not all Gypsies wish to settle in houses, and there are still groups who travel and live on unlawful sites. Here the Gypsies are left to their traditional occupations, dealing in scrap metal and hawking their wares, until they too are permanently settled. Apart from these groups and the families that occasionally wander across the border from Berkshire, there are no longer any real travellers in Hampshire. They have been overtaken by the new conditions of our society and forced to adjust to them. Though they have gained in some ways, these Gypsies have finally lost their old life style, however difficult it was. With it they have lost their freedom and their true identity, and these are losses which impoverish the cultural life of us all, and which can only be a cause for regret.

It is difficult today to visualize the Gypsy life of even seventy years ago when most families travelled, spoke their own language, pursued their traditional occupations and rigidly observed their ancient customs. This way of life has practically disappeared and in Hampshire most of the Gypsy population has been settled permanently in council housing. But at the end of the last century one could still find Gypsies in tents and wagons at Shave Green, Godshill, Copythorne, Longdown, Thorney Hill, Bransgore and other places deep in the Forest. Their history has been remembered and re-told by Ruth Lavender (1986) and M.W.Penfold (1991)

The Story of Thorney Hill
In the middle of the nineteenth century the hamlet of Thorney Hill consisted of a few thatched cottages and a colony of Romanies living on top of the hill in tents, in the holly bushes on the edge of the New Forest. Some travelling workers came to the hamlet to work on the brick kilns. The Romanies lived a hard life making clothes pegs, besom brooms and giving a service with their knife grinding machines in neighbouring villages. Their whippets caught rabbits. Their way of life is depicted by carvings on some gravestones in the Church graveyard.

Drunk in charge cases at Christchurch are no new phenomena. Just a century ago a Thorney Hill man was, in the space of a few days, fined three times for being drunk in charge of horses at Christchurch and Bransgore. No loss of licence apparently. This chap, and members of his family, were at about the same time regularly penalised for furious driving (of a horse, of course) in Christchurch High Street, for driving a cart round and round Ringwood market place, for drunkenness, assaults and other misdemeanours.

The family's story is just one of many told by Ruth Lavender in *The Story Of Thorney Hill* (1986). Perhaps, unfortunately for the friends of Thorney Hill, some of the best documented material is about the various misdemeanours of its residents over the years. Mrs Lavender has a complete chapter devoted to this, which includes references to Gypsies:

"John Pidgeley was fined in 1879 for letting a donkey stray on the road; Andrew James drunk in 1880; in 1884 John Pateman was sentenced for beating a horse to make it go faster and faster when he was drunk; in 1886 Noah Burton was given the choice of a 30s. fine or 14 days in prison for stealing George Skew's coat left on his horse at *Picket Post Inn*; in 1886, and again in 1889, John Burton, a Gypsy, was fined for allowing his horse to stray on the road. He argued that he thought it was alright if the beasts were tethered or had a boy in charge; in 1889 John Pidgeley drunk in charge of a horse and brick trunk only a few days after being fined for damaging Charles Vatcher's door; in 1890 George Scott and Harriett James for horses found as far off as North Bockhampton Road; Charlotte James was fined in 1890 for leaving a horse and cart unattended in Purewell."

Thorney Hill had a Gypsy camp site and has long been associated with them. Over 300 attended a Gypsy funeral there not so long ago. But Gypsy members fell rapidly and many of those remaining intermarried with the general community. Squatters occupied huts at Holmsley South built for the RAF crews of planes who flew from the nearby Holmsley Airfield in the last war. Mrs Lavender makes it clear that these residents weren't necessarily undesirable. Certainly the Gypsies were friendly and scrupulously honest with those who treated them well:

"When Gypsies ceased to be allowed to camp wherever they lived in the New Forest one of the sites allotted to them was at Thorney Hill crossroads on the land east of the road to Burley and north of Forest Road. Although called a compound it was never fenced. It was the largest Gypsy community in the New Forest, probably 400 at its most populous, and after mains water was laid on in the 1930s it had one tap. Nevertheless there was always a lot of washing spread out over the bushes to dry.

By the 1950's Gypsy members had greatly declined and they had inter-married with non-Romany families to such an extent that they were known locally as didecai. (One highly respectable Romany, settled in a council house in Burnt House Lane, scornfully called them 'tinkers'). The 45 children who went to a party given for them by the Women's Institute at Christmas 1934 came from families of Smith, Lamb, Doe, Sherrard, Pidgeley, James, Moore and Williams. Later the leading family were the Hughes, which they always pronounced Yews.

Horse coping had gone out by the 1950s, but there was always a good deal of scrap iron lying round the compound. Women pushing old prams collected wood for their fires and begged housewives for rag, by which they meant old clothes. They adopted a special voice for begging, but if you asked them not to the word was passed round and you were addressed in a normal voice thereafter. They bought most of their clothes at jumble sales.

They appreciated and reciprocated kindness and resented contempt. The gardens of the kindly were so safe that John Lavender, giving a couple of lads a lift across the Forest, learnt from their conversation that they knew his two acres as well as he did, but nothing was ever stolen from it. But the unfriendly might lose all their daffodil flowers, which were sold along with bog myrtle from the Forest in a nearby town.

Before Christmas they gathered and sold holly and butchers' broom from the Forest and mistletoe which must have come from somewhere. If a child was lost they would turn out and hunt for it, and their own children were always very quiet on buses and in public places.

They were physically strong. They would walk all the way to Purwell labour exchange and back. On buses the women were recognisable not only by their appearance but by their enormous baskets, about two feet long by one foot across, and by the ease with which they carried their heavy loads of shopping. Another instance occurred in Christchurch High Street. A very heavy motorcycle, propped against the curb, was knocked by a passer-by and immediately seized by Mrs Cooper's spare hand and held steady, no mean feat. Its owner slipped her a florin but she insisted on his taking some of her flowers in return.

They had their own funeral customs. The last time a caravan was burnt on the death of its owner must have been in the late 1950s, but keening during the funeral service was continued by some families long after that, as was the practice of the widow feigning to throw herself into the open grave and being restrained by the mourners.

Before the coffin lid was screwed down there was a ceremonial leave taking, a kiss or a touch, by individual friends and relatives, supervised by the local "queen". They never came into the church before the funeral but lined up in twos and followed the coffin.

When the local 'king', Mr Hughes, died in the 1960s over 300 attended, many of them from elsewhere. Not all could get into the church but some were crammed into the organ gallery and were so excited that the organist was afraid someone would fall over the balustrade into the crowd below.

As soon as a funeral was over everyone became very cheerful and on that particular occasion men sat about on the road verges for the rest of the day, drinking beer until the supplies at the off-licence ran out. The Sunday following a funeral the closest female relatives, dressed in black, attended the regular morning service, though they never came at other times.

Although funeral expenses always had to be paid by the state, there would be enormous numbers of beautiful wreaths, which on one occasion showed considerable light heartedness. Just before Christmas a man had been drinking and when he got to a friend's house he sat down and died. At least one full bottle was thrown into his grave and a spectacular wreath was made round a whiskey bottle.

There was some serious poverty. About 1963 Marjorie McLeish was horrified when her husband, Dr Alistair McLeish, visited a Gypsy family on Christmas Eve and found they had no food whatever. Shortly afterwards she learnt that a Gypsy child had said to its mother, 'Father Christmas didn't bring me anything. Do you think, if I'm very good, he will next year?' It went to Marjorie's heart. She coped with the foodless family right away and the next Christmas saw the beginning of 'Marjorie's Christmas Parcels.'

As her generosity became known her friends supported her, and very soon the big strawboard boxes, covered with brightly coloured Christmas paper, contained a chicken and a pudding for each family, bacon, sausages, potatoes, cabbages, fruit, jam, trinkets for the older girls, and at least one toy per child.

The excitement when she delivered the parcels was immense and one young helper found that his job was to stand guard over the car to prevent the deliriously happy children helping themselves. A few families had very little brain; to begin with Majorie supplied the chickens raw, but when she found one or two families were throwing them away because they did not know how to cook them, she roasted the lot herself.

By about 1960 most of the last number of squatters, who had occupied the Nissen huts at Holmsley, about a mile away, when the RAF moved out at the end of the war, had been properly housed, and the Hampshire County Council gave its attention to the Forest Gypsies. It was decided that they must all come off the Forest and be put into council houses. To prepare them for this the council erected 22 second hand prefabricated houses on the site of the compound, provided a road, Thorney Hill Close, water and electricity, stopped the use of shacks, caravans and tents, cleaned the site, moved the families into the houses, and appointed a warden and social workers to help them.

An attractive wooden bus shelter was erected near the crossroads in 1959 but vandalism was so bad that it was removed in 1963. The following year Miss Swift, the welfare officer working for the Gypsies on the edge of the Forest, persuaded the Council to put it back but by the end of 1972 it had been so badly damaged that it was again removed.

As families were moved into permanent houses, their prefabs were demolished to prevent squatters moving in. Heating in their shacks took the form of a fire in an oil drum in the middle of the shack with a stovepipe going up through the roof. They found houses heated by a fire 'in the wall' very cold.

By the end of 1974 all but the four most difficult families had gone. The warden and social worker were withdrawn and these families, abandoned on a derelict site, their old way of life and their own community totally destroyed, not surprisingly, became seriously anti-social. The vandalism they committed was frightening.

Even the rule of never injuring the kindly flew to the winds: old Eleanor Willis at Moorland Cottage had her bedroom window smashed one night and was too terrified even to telephone for help; and the Lakes at Forest Corner, who had always in a quiet way tried to help the didecai, had their bungalow damaged. Burley School was broken into and robbed.

Ignited bottles of petrol were thrown at the cars of the genuinely unfriendly. An unoccupied cottage was broken into and its furniture wrecked. And so on. As Chairman of the Parish Council and a sincere well-wisher of the Gypsies, Marjorie McLeish did her utmost to get them re-housed, but she died at the end of 1975 unsuccessful, and it was still many months before they were resettled, at Ibsley.

Apart from this tragic last couple of years, the Gypsies were generally pretty well behaved. Until the 1960s people could and did leave doors and windows open when they went out, and even after that it was outsiders, not the local inhabitants, who forced them to lock up carefully. There were a few exceptions. One of the Hughes was imprisoned for a near murderous attack on another Hughes. And there was an incomparable character, a small, dark, quiet, politely spoken woman, who after nine children (by more than one father) was persuaded that this was enough, and subsequently informed her friends that she had been 'pasteurised'.

Sometimes on the long, hot trek up the hill from Bransgore she would call at Heather Lodge and ask for a drink of water for herself and one or two small children walking with her and some milk for the baby in its pram; and she would pull out an unwrapped teat for the baby bottle from her pocket. In spite of this her children always appeared healthy and physically well cared for. But towards the end they were a wild lot; taken into care they would be in trouble with the police within days of coming home again.

Her misdemeanours included breaking into a holiday-maker's caravan on the Forest. When caught in the act she very nearly convinced the owners that she was helping the police with their enquiries, and the newspaper report of what she said had readers convulsed with laughter. She used someone else's child allowance book once and though illiterate herself was able to present a forged prescription for a pain killer after Dr McLeish had refused to prescribe more unless she went to a dentist first. Finally, alas, she went too far and assaulted two of the staff at Bransgore School and had a spell in Holloway Prison, whence she emerged with new clothes and her hair 'permed' but otherwise unaltered. Life at Thorney Hill was safer after her removal to Ibsley but much less amusing."

The book is illustrated with an 1869 Ordnance Survey map of Thorney Hill and several photographs, including the Methodist Chapel, the school, the site of the Gypsy compound and later prefabs, and All Saints church.

Thorney Hill This, That and T'Other
M.W. Penfold (1991) also recorded many memories of the Thorney Hill Gypsies: "There have been families camping on the Forest for many generations. The Romanies with their beautifully painted wagons and skilled crafts used the Forest as a temporary resting place, before moving on. They would trade anything on four legs, but had a soft spot for 'coloured' horses. They earned money selling articles they had made, and doing odd jobs.

Then there were those who made a more permanent camp in benders. Even these could be re-erected, put on a cart and moved, making an instant caravan. Benders consisted of saplings pushed into the ground at about 6-8ft apart and tied together. Several of these would be put together to form a tunnel, closed in one end, and a ridge pole along the centre would hold them in place. Some folks managed to obtain a tarpaulin, others would make do with blankets and anything else handy. Smoke from the fire would help to make them waterproof in time.

Food was plentiful in the Forest, and the youngsters soon learned the art of catching rabbits, pigeons, squirrels, hedgehogs and pheasants. The big cooking pot would hang over the fire on a kettle crane, and meat and vegetables would all be put in together. Water had to be carried from the nearest well, which no doubt was a job for the older children. Washing was hung on the bushes to dry.

In the spring the travellers would pack up their belongings and set off 'up country'. The call would sound across the Forest 'See you in the hop country'. They'd pick up casual jobs on the way, always doing an honest day's work. Some would head for the strawberry fields around Southampton, others towards Winchester. The hop fields were the ultimate destination, and potato picking was done where there was a need. With the arrival of a cattle lorry in the village, they were taken to the hop fields in style.

As the autumn drew near, they would wend their way back to the shelter of the Forest, and make a living where we would probably starve. From the Forestry Commission they could obtain a ticket for a shilling, permitting them to cut holly for wreaths, collect moss for the florists' shops. If there was a year in which holly berries were in short supply, they'd soak dried peas, paint them red and wire them together in bunches.

The travellers' clothes pegs are well known and still around today. Making them was a family concern, each doing a bit to help. They would obtain the every day items used by families, bootlaces, matches, pins, and these would be taken round from house to house. Some could make chrysanthemum flowers from whittling a stick, and no doubt many a carving was done round the camp fire. Besoms, beeskips, 'nikki' wood from kindling, 'black jacks' for fire lighting, all came from the Forest.

The women were renowned for flower selling. They'd walk for miles to nurseries to buy flowers, then take them to the local town to sell. Of course wild flowers were picked by the children and made into posies for the ladies to buy. When buses made their appearance in Thorney Hill, and the roads were in better condition, several Thorney Hill people would be regular customers on the Saturday morning bus, baskets loaded with flowers. The last of these was Mrs Jeff in the 1950s; she had a regular selling place in Christchurch for years.

A friend of mine related a gem of a story about a family of van dwellers passing through the Forest in the area of Emery Down. These travellers consider it unlucky to call a child by its name before it is christened. So they decided to see the Vicar of the nearest church. During the service he asked the name of the child. 'Rizver' he was told. Thinking he hadn't heard properly, he asked again. So the child was duly christened Rizver. On making the entry in the baptismal book he requested the origin of this rather unusual named. 'Please sir, don't ye mind they's making a place on the top of the hill to hold water for Lyndhurst, and they calls it Rizver, so I thought as how it would be a nice name for my little boy.' The Vicar was greatly amused, and so the story is told about the Reservoir baby of Lyndhurst.

In the evenings the travellers would gather round. Tommy Cooper had a 'squeeze box' and would soon have them singing and dancing. There is an old song, no doubt passed down:

I'm a Romany Rye, a true didicai,
That's how they call me a Romany Rye.
I live in a tent, and don't pay no rent
That's why they call me a Romany Rye.

When the travellers were on the road, they would camp near a farmstead. The farmers often had work for them. One tale I was told of two travellers talking over their journey on meeting up again. 'I managed to find one horse, Bill,' the man said, 'but I had to hunt for t'other; she'd ate herself into the hayrick, and I had a job to get her out.' He had a pair of big roan horses, and I imagine when he saw the hole in the rick he soon left that area".

The "unique photographs" in this book include building the church at Thorney Hill, Thorney Hill school photographs (1920 and 1929), the war memorial, bygones (including travellers' clothes pegs) and a little chavie waiting for breakfast.

There are several sketch maps by G. Anders including four of Thorney Hill: "dwellings in existence around 1910" indicates where the "forest dwellers" lived, near "Devils walk", a path which connected Forest Road, via the hollies, to the Burley Road; "dwellings in existence in 1991" shows that Thorney Hill has not changed substantially in over eighty years; "roads and tracks around 1810" shows how Thorney Hill was connected to Burley, Bransgore and other places; "Thorney Hill 1900" shows the brickfields and kilns of Thorney Hill. There are also maps of Holmsley as at 1939-1940 and Holmsley South Aerodrome 1942-1946.

There are several delightful sketches by Mrs P Smith including: the churchyard at All Saints before the gales of 1990, the Methodist Chapel, the school, the off licence and cottages.

Postscript
On 19 February 2003 a report was presented to Hampshire County Council on "Capital funding for voluntary village halls and community centres – Thorney Hill". This report was seeking approval to spend £26,350 on a new village hall at Thorney Hill:

"This area of the New Forest is isolated through lack of transport and no longer has within it other local amenities. It has lost communal buildings and services in recent years including the village school, post office and local shop. A proportion of the population originate from Forest Gypsies who have been in settled housing for the last twenty to thirty years". (Hampshire County Council, 2003)

5. Strewing the Pateran

"Again the scene changes, and one is standing on the open common, amid a troop of raklos who are riding up a drove of rough Forest ponies, whilst a buxom rakli holds up the sod of grass with which she is 'Strewing the Pateran' for the rest of the tribe, some of whom are already following up the trail behind the oaks and hollies. There is another story woven in with this picture, of a silver ring worn on the artist's hand and a secret kept for sixteen years. But this you must learn from the painter herself some day."

Baptisms and births are important signs on the pateran trail. The parish of Bransgore was created in 1874 from Christchurch and Sopley. However, the baptism and burial registers commence earlier, from 1822. There are no transcripts, but burials 1822-1837 are in the Hampshire Genealogical Society Burial Index.

The early baptism records for Christchurch are very hard to read but there is a baptism recorded on 10 March 1813 for what looks like Mary Pateman, daughter of William and Jane. Another hard to read entry looks like the baptism on 23 October 1814 of Eliza Pateman, daughter of William and Elizabeth.

Given that the distinctive name of Major appears in the New Forest Pateman family, it is interesting to note that Elizabeth Jane Major was baptized on 25 June 1820. Her parents were William and Mary.

Then there are the Pitmans, who may or may not be Patemans. John and Elizabeth Pitman had two children baptized: Frances on 3 March 1823 and Elizabeth on 2 April 1825. Isaac and Charlotte Pitman had baptisms for four children: Lydia (24 May 1833), George (24 August 1834), Emma (September 1835) and Selina (4 March 1838) Job and Louisa Pitman had two children baptized: Dorothy (2 May 1897) and Alice Amelia (13 December 1905). Jon and Betsy Pitman had one child baptized: Alice Amelia (2 November 1924). Another Pitman baptism took place on 3 October 1926, the child of Job and Elizabeth Pitman.

But our family history starts for sure on 10 June 1832 with the baptism of Charles Pateman at Woodmancote. His parents were Jane and John Pateman, a travelling basket maker from Toddington in Bedfordshire. Their previous child, William, had been baptised at Bisham in Berkshire on 9 May 1830. Bisham is actually just over the river from Marlow. For some quirky reason, a lot of Marlow people were baptized in Bisham and vice versa. Although the name Pateman is more often found in the north of the county, it does appear in the south as well, and also in Buckinghamshire. John and Jane may have had at least two more sons – Major and Sidney Pateman – and a daughter, Peggy Pateman (aka Margaret Curtis) who was baptised at Salisbury in 1828. Sharon Flaote: "Peg or Margaret Pateman alias Curtis of Bedfordshire, wife of Frank Doe of Hampshire – this reference comes partly from the 1881 census index and partly from an oral history source recorded in the Gypsy collection at the University of Liverpool".

William Pateman (born at Bisham, 1830) married Mary Ann James (from another travelling family) and their first child, William, was baptised at Beaulieu in 1848. The family later settled at Thorney Hill. If you mark Toddington, Bisham, Woodmancote, and Beaulieu on a map you will notice that it is almost possible to connect them with a straight line. This line marks the journey of the Pateman family from Bedfordshire to the New Forest. Other branches of the Pateman family – including my own – made a similar journey from Bedfordshire to other parts of England (in my case, to Kent).

Sharon Floate: "I've always understood that 'Pateman' as a Gypsy name tends to be found in Bedfordshire and neighbouring counties. Is this where your family tended to travel?" Other Bedfordshire baptisms include: Thomas Pateman (1790), William and Ann, Haughton; Thomas Pateman (1793), John and Elizabeth, Wooton; Thomas Pateman (1795), George and Hannah, Langford; Thomas Pateman (1799), Michael and Elizabeth, Todington. Elizabeth Pateman was baptised at Flitwick, Bedfordshire, on 16 August 1807 (born 15 April). The parents were John and Susan, "travelling chairbottomers". Major Pateman, son of Mary and Michoel (sic) "of Toddington, labourer" was baptised on 18 August 1872 at Toddington.

William (basket maker) and Mary Ann had nine more children: George (1850), Olive / Nell (1852), Mary Ann (1853), Matilda (1854), John (1856), Job (1859), Thomas (1860), Mary Jane (1863) and John (1878). Some of these were baptised at Holybourne and Binstead during the hop picking season: Olive and Matilda, for example, were baptised at Holybourne on 20 August 1854 and Mary Jane was baptised on 13 September 1863 at Binstead.

Eddie Higgins: "My great grandmother was Matilda Pateman and came from Thorney Hill in the New Forest. My great grandfather, Henry Osborne was born in Stow Uplands, Suffolk. They are shown on the 1891 census as living in Shoreditch. Henry was 24, Matilda was 25. She stated her birth place as Ferwood in Dorset but on the 1901 census she says she was born in Thorny Wood, Hants. In 1901 they were living at Somerford St, Bethnal Green. Their children were: Harry (24), William, (19), George (16), Lilian (12), Charles (9), Albert (5)."

Also baptised on 13 September 1863 at Binstead was Olive Pateman, daughter of Major Pateman (basket maker) and Louisa Doe (from another travelling family) of Lymington. Their previous child, Harriett, had been baptised at Binstead on 28 September 1862.

Major Pateman may have been a brother (or other relative) to William Pateman (born at Bisham in 1830). Similarly, Sidney Pateman may also have been a brother or relative to both William and Major Pateman. All three of them were basket makers and had children baptised at Holybourne or Binstead during the 1860s.

Sidney was married to Louisa and they had two children baptised at Binstead during the hop season: Sidney (16 September 1866) and Peter (8 September 1868).

A number of Pateman baptisms took place at the Wesleyan Methodist Chapel at Thorney Hill, which was heavily used by the local Gypsy community. William and Elizabeth Pateman had three children baptised in this chapel: Mary Jane (19 November 1877), Caroline (16 February 1879) and Frank (16 February 1897). John and Rowena Pateman had two children baptised at the chapel: Ralph John (11 November 1878) and Walter George (16 February 1879). Ralph John and Mary Jane Pateman's son, John was baptised in this chapel on 30 March 1902.

The Pateman family tradition of baptisms at Holybourne / Binstead during the hop picking season was carried on by Job and Thomas Pateman. Job (hawker) and Louisa's child, Patience, was baptised at Binstead on 22 September 1878; George, was baptised at Kinson on 25 October 1886. Kinson is near the New Forest and close to the West Moors Gypsy encampment / settlement.

Thomas (hawker) and Matilda had two children, Ellen Mary and Caroline, baptised at Binstead on 14 September 1884; Alice Louisa, was baptised at Christchurch (Twynham) on 5 September 1886; and Emily was baptised at Burley, in the New Forest, close to their home at Thorney Hill, on 18 June 1888.

From 1891 most of the Pateman baptisms were at Thorney Hill, starting with Thomas (Gipsy labourer) and Matilda's daughter, Ethel, on 11 May 1891. Others included George Pateman (son of William and Elizabeth) on 13 March 1901 and George Henry Pateman (son of Ralph John and Mary Jane) on 26 February 1905.

Census

The Census gives us more clues. No Patemans appeared in the 1841 Census at either Woodmancote or Burley, so we do not know where John and Jane Pateman were after the baptism of their son Charles at Woodmancote in 1832.

There are no Patemans in the 1851 Census for Hampshire, but there are a number of Pitmans. There are three Pitman families: William and Mary Ann from Hursley had three children; Isaac and Charlotte from Hursley and Winkton had six children; and John and Elizabeth from Burley had three children. Living alone were Emma Pitman from Hursley, and Lydia Pitman from Burley.

The 1861 Census for Thorney Hill shows the family of William (born at Bisham in 1830) and Mary Ann "Peatman". They have seven children and a lodger, John Dough (Doe). This family also appears on the Census for 1871, 1881, and 1891.

In 1871 Job Pateman was travelling with Nehemiah Doe and his family. Lesley Doe: "Nehemiah Doe was my great great grandfather. I have not come across a marriage yet for him and his supposed wife Ruth." This is a reference to Nehemiah Doe (1834-1911) and Rose Ruth Jeff (1850-1918). According to Sue Day "Nehemiah and Rose Ruth travelled all over the country, from Hampshire right up to Hertfordshire and Oxford, travelling through Dorset, Wiltshire, Bristol and Somerset to name only a few".

Also on the 1881 Census are the families of three of William's children: John (and Rowena, also on the 1891 census), William (and Elizabeth, also on the 1891 and 1901 Census) and Job (and Louisa, also on the 1891 Census). In 1881, Mary A. Pateman (17, Christchurch) was living with Matthew Jeff and his family at Thorney Hill. Mary Pateman married John Jeff in 1902.

Another of William's children, Thomas (and Matilda) appear on the 1891 and 1901 Census. In 1891 Harry Pateman (8, nephew, Thorney Hill) was living with Sidney James and his family at Thorney Hill. In 1901 Harry Pateman (lodger, Thorney Hill) was living with James Scott and his family in a tent at Thorney Hill.

The Passing Through website also lists some Patemans who were born in Hampshire and travelling at the time of the 1891 census. These included Joseph Pateman (40, travelling Gypsy, Hants, Basingstoke) his wife Mary Pateman (37, Hants, Andover) and their children, Ada Pateman (19, Andover), Siberina Pateman (20, Andover) and Shipton Pateman (1, Andover), who were living at Park Downs, Banstead, Surrey.

Marriages

Marriages provide us with additional information. The first recorded marriage was that of Naomi Bateman (or Peatman, 1809-1890), who married William Doe (1807-1890) at Lasham on 22 July 1834. Lesley Doe: "My great great great grandfather was supposedly married to Naomi Bateman (Peatman, Pateman)". John Pateman married Mary Pateman at Wallisdown on 21 January 1901.

The first marriage at Bransgore, All Saints, Thorney Hill was on 27 October 1902 between Mary Pateman and John Jeff. She was the daughter of Thomas and Matilda Pateman. One of the witnesses was Mary's sister, Alice, who married Frederick White on 24 April 1905. Another sister, Emily, was a witness.

Mary Jane Pateman married Bertie Broomfield (a very big Thorney Hill family) on 10 September 1904. Mary's parents were William and Elizabeth Pateman. The fathers of both the bride and groom were brickmakers, which was a major industry in Thorney Hill at this time. The witnesses included two of Mary's siblings, George and Caroline Pateman.

In his book *On the Gypsy Trail*, Alan McGowan points out that "marriage was frequently, though not exclusively, to members of other travelling families…families travelling in Hampshire included…Pateman". Another New Forest family mentioned by MacGowan is the Doe family and there were many connections between the Pateman and Doe families.

Stephen Doe: "Patience Pateman married Henry Doe (born 20/05/1874) in Stratfield Saye, although there is no record yet of their marriage. I guess they jumped the broom stick! Patience Doe died on 26 June 1960 while living on Hayling Island and she is buried at St Mary's church there. Henry Doe died on 18 July 1943 and is buried in the same grave." Stephen sent me a photograph of Patience and Henry Doe sitting outside their vardo, possibly in the Southampton area.

Patience and Henry had nine children: Alice Doe (born 1897, Turget) married her cousin William Doe (born 1898); Patience Doe (born 28/10/1898, Bramely) married John Henry Cooper (born 1898) on 5 August 1918 in St Marks Church, Talbot. They had eight children; Henry Doe [Stephen's great grandfather] (born 29/01/1900, Sunningdale, Surrey) married Selina Cooper (born 25/03/1902) at Southampton on 18 December 1922. Henry died on 7 August 1976 and Lena died on 7 August 1978; Britannia Doe (born 1906, Clutton) married Nelson Stokes [possibly related to Louisa Stokes?] with 3 children; Nelson Doe (born 1910, Farnham) married Milly Rickman, they had seven children; Job Doe (born 1914, Alton) married Rosie Saxby and had three children; William Doe married Janey Keets with two children; Louisa Doe married George Jones with 4 children; John Doe married Mary Scot with three children.

Henry and Selina Doe had nine children, including Stephen's grandfather, Liberty Doe (born 09/09/1930). Liberty Doe had two children, Nickolas and Stuart (Stephen's father). Stuart Doe married Denise Hazel and they had four children – Lisa, Julia, Hannah and Stephen.

Lesley Doe: "Edith Pateman (daughter of Job and Louisa) was the wife of William Doe (baptised 1851). They had three children: Willie (23 May 1898), Job (27 July 1900) and Rosie (born 25 June 1901, died 21 August 1901)."

Janet Keet-Black: "My late aunt and her husband Teddy Doe (real name Pateman) lived at Thorney Hill before moving into a council bungalow at Bransgore".

Robert Dawson: "Bella Cooper was nee Pike, daughter of a Doe and a Pateman. A man called Pateman was a day labourer in the New Forest in 1911".

Another family with close ties to the Patemans was the White family: Alice Louisa Pateman married Frederick White in 1905; John Pateman married Sarah White in 1923; Rose Pateman married Leonard White in 1930.

Deaths and burials
The final clues on our pateran trail can be found on death and burial certificates and gravestones. The first recorded death was that of Jane Pateman at Lymington in 1858. This could have been the wife of John Pateman (from Toddington) and the mother of William (1830) and Charles (1832). The first burial at Thorney Hill was of George Pateman on 27 February 1864. This was followed by John (1 March 1881), William (9 April 1886), John (28 March 1887), William (12 February 1892), Infant daughter of Rose Pateman (13 March 1893), and Mary Pateman (7 April 1909).

After All Saints church was built, many of the Patemans were buried in the churchyard there, including: Alfred (2 October 1918), Elizabeth (24 April 1922), Job (16 July 1923), Thomas (30 April 1929), William (14 September 1937) and Ralph John (1 February 1945).

A Novel Gipsy Village in the New Forest
Newspaper articles provide clues on the pateran trail, such as this item which appeared in the *Morning Leader* on 3 June 1907:

"Gypsies are so generally regarded as a race of nomad undesirables that it is interesting to learn of a village whose respectable and well behaved citizens are mainly of the Gypsy race.

The population of the little village of Thorny Hill, on the outskirts of the New Forest, has for many years past consisted principally of Gypsies, who now number about 100. Most of the original inhabitants have long since departed, and the few Hampshire rustics who have not forsaken the homes of their forefathers, scarcely regard their fellow villagers as aliens nowadays, and marriages between the two races are not of uncommon occurrence. As a rule it is the 'native' men who fall victims to the charms of the Gypsy girls.

Caravans are rarely to be seen at Thorny Hill, for the Gypsies live in typical English thatched cottages, and have almost completely adapted themselves to a settled life; but now and again the restless Romany blood makes itself felt in springtime, and a family or two get 'on the move', to return to the comforts of indoor life when the summer is over. But for the most part the Gypsies remain at Thorny Hill all the year round. They have their share, too, of the comforts and amenities of civilisation. There is the village shop, where everything in reason may be bought, a school, and two places of worship. The little white church, with its whiter stone approach, reminds one of a sort of toy Taj Mahal. This church is a chapel-of –ease to that of the neighbouring village of Bransgore, from which it is served. It was built a year ago by Lord and Lady Manners in memory of their daughter.

All the Gypsies have adopted English names, Scott and Pateman being the favourites; and the Scotts are so numerous as to comprise nearly half the entire population. The families are very clannish, and it is quite common to find three generations living together in the same cottage. The elder women still cling to the picturesque Romany head dress, but the others have adopted the conventional hat. Ear rings are, however, still de rigueur for both sexes.

The women of the community do most in the way of earning a living, for they journey to Bournemouth – they call it Bourne – on Tuesdays, Thursdays, and Saturdays, with great baskets of flowers to sell in the streets. Their men folk often drive them in little carts drawn by New Forest ponies to Christchurch, about eight miles distant; thence they travel by train to Bournemouth, the return journey costing them 6d. A woman will often pay as much as £2 for the day's supply of flowers, so that the risk is considerable, especially in wet weather. Still, on the whole they do a good business, especially in the holiday season when Bournemouth is flooded with visitors, who can rarely resist them, especially if they happen to be carrying a little brown baby as well as their big basket of flowers.

The Gypsies keep their own cows, which roam about the commons, and also commandeer the New Forest ponies, many of which are now quite tame. It is a great sight to see the little procession of carts returning home from Christchurch at full gallop, the cares of the day forgotten, and the Gypsies laughing and chatting over their experiences. Altogether the Gypsy village is not the least of the many charms of the New Forest."

There are three photographs accompanying this article, captioned: "The Little White Church at Thorny Hill", "A Gypsy Flower Seller" and "A Typical Gypsy Cottage."

This article was also published in the *Christchurch Times* (15 June 1907) and the *Northern Echo*, Darlington (10 July 1907).

Bad Language
Hampshire Post 7 June 1907: "Robert Pateman, Gypsy, was summoned for using obscene language on Sunday May 26. P.C. Manuel stated that the defendant was in Southampton Road, Park Gate, Sarisbury, when he made use of the language complained of. He advised the defendant to go to his camp, whereupon he took off his coat and said he could fight 40 policemen. A fine of £1 and costs was imposed.

Sydney Pateman, a brother of the last defendant, was summoned for a like offence, at the same time and place, and was likewise fined £1 and costs."

Soon after these articles appeared, Sidney Pateman was baptised on 28 July 1907 at Locks Heath. His parents were Mary Anne and Sidney Pateman, a traveller from Sarisbury. Three more children were to follow: Charles Henry Pateman, baptised on 4 April 1909 at Park Gate, Sarisbury; Mary Ann Pateman, baptised on 4 July 1915 at Swanwick; and Rose Pateman, baptised on 27 July 1917, also at Swanwick.

Alice Gillington
Articles in the the *Journal of the Gypsy Lore Society* also contain a number of signs on the pateran trail. The article about Amelia Goddard, *The House of the Open Door* by Alice Gillington (1908), refers to the singing of a famous Gypsy ballad, "The Three Gypsies": "This ballad, a variant of The Gypsy Laddie, and concerned, as the words 'yellow castle's' (Earl of Cassillis') in the last line indicate, with the elopement of the Countess of Cassillis and Johnny Faa, is more complete than another version collected from English Gypsies by Mr Sampson (*J.G.L.S.*, Old Series, ii. 84-5). The words and melody, as sung at Thorney Hill, Hants, in July 1908, by Thomas Pateman, a middle-aged Gypsy, are as follows:

There was three Gypsies all in a row,
And they sang brisk and bonny, O!
They sang so high, and they sang so low,
Till downstairs came the lady, O!

They gave to she a nut-a-meg brown,
And a cake of the very best ginger, O!
But she gave to them a far better thing,
For she gave them the ring from her finger, O!

Now she pulled off her silken gown,
And she wrapped the blanket round her, O!
She was resolved and rakeish too,
To gang with the draggle-tail Gypsies, O!

When her new lord he did return
Enquiring for his lady, O!
One of the servants did say, 'Sir,
She's gone with the draggle-tail Gypsies, O!'

Come saddle me my milk-white steed,
Come saddle me my pony, O!
That I might ride both day and night
Until I find my lady, O!

O, he rode high and he rode low,
And he rode over the valley, O!
And who should he see but his own wedded lady
Along with the draggle-tail Gypsies, O!

Now how could you leave your house and land?
How could you leave your babes also?
Or how could you leave your new-wedded lord
To gang with the draggle-tail Gypsies, O?

Last night you laid on a good feather-bed,
Along with your tender babes also!
And now tonight in a cold open field,
Along with the draggle-tail Gypsies, O!

I will return to my house and land;
I will return to my babes also!
And I will return to my new-wedded lord,
And forsake all the draggle-tail Gypsies, O!

Now there was three Gypsies all of a row,
And they was hanged all just so;
And they was hanged all of a row
For stealing the yellow castle's lady, O!"

The Thomas Pateman who sang this ballad died on 27 April 1929 and was buried at All Saints, Thorney Hill, on 30 April 1929. His funeral was reported in *The Christchurch Times* on 4 May 1929. "Thomas Pateman died at his home at Forest Side, Thorney Hill on Saturday April the 27th, aged 69. Mourners at the funeral were: Mrs Pateman, widow; Mr W. Pateman, brother; Mrs G Burton, sister, Bella, Maisie and Will; Mrs Jeff, Mrs Greggory, Mrs Feltham, Mrs Turner, daughters; Mr G Jeff, Mr F White, Mr E Greggory, Mr C Feltham, son in laws; Prissie, Henry, Alice, Freddy, Tom, Tilley, Charles, Doris, May and Bill, grandchildren; Caroline, Hetty, Joe, Lily, Rose, Alice, Jane and Nore, cousins; Mr R Burton and Mr H Burton, brothers in law; Mrs N Burton and Mrs Louisa Pateman, sisters in law".

Henry Gibbins
Henry Gibbins ran "the New Forest Good Samaritan Charity" which provided housing, rent paid, and a stock of prepaid groceries on a weekly basis to poor people in the New Forest. Most of his clients were elderly Gypsies, including the famous queen Hannah Lakey, who died in 1903 but who's photo by John Golden Short is still available as a post card today. It must be the most seen of all Gypsy pictures – an old woman with white coal scuttle bonnet, with a swiggler.

In 1909 Gibbins wrote *Gipsies of the New Forest and Other Tales*. This book, by and large, though fairly patronising, has some good information about New Forest Gypsies of the time. His attitude towards Gypsies was generally neutral, perhaps even slightly favourable, although his intentions were obviously toward assimilation rather than emancipation. He thought that a European conference on Gypsies would be a good idea because it would give them due attention, even though the aim of the conference was not sympathetic to their cause:

"I see by the papers of the day (January 1908) that a conference of the European Powers is to be held this year on the Continent, with a view to doing away with the

Gypsy element – or plague, as they call it – and that Great Britain has promised to send delegates." The UK Aliens Act was passed in 1909.

Gibbins noted a decline in the Gypsy population: 'Lakey, Sherred, Doe, Sherrard, Sherwin, Sherwood, Wells, Blake, Green, Wareham, Barnes, Peters, Cooper, Pateman, White, Pearce, Miles, Rose, Stone, etc. The Stanleys and Lees have quite died out in these parts during the last few years.'

'It is not the home to them it used to be. What with the venison, game, and rabbits, which abounded in the Forest, and at all times kept the stock pot well supplied, and a little good liquor, 'smuggled spirits', truly it was a paradise to them. No rent, no rates, or taxes, good food and firing gratis, and health unbought; it might well swarm with nomads, or, as they always call themselves, - Travellers'.

Gibbin's book contains a map of 24 New Forest Gypsy sites and stopping places. These include "Thorney Hill, amongst the holly bushes". A review of *Gypsies of the New Forest and Other Tales* was published in the *Journal of the Gypsy Lore Society* in 1909:

"The New Forest is no longer a Gypsy paradise where an abundance of food and firewood can be had for the taking, and smuggled liquor almost for the asking. Fortunate thieves who have already stolen half its area are diligent to curtail their privileges of the less fortunate, squadrons of trippers infest its glades throughout the summer months, its deer have been destroyed by Act of Parliament, and its wild inhabitants are being compelled to quit a manner of life which the Gajo has made illegal.

But the Gajo has not thought fit to provide for them an honest means of livelihood which they can adopt without violence to their instincts. And so the Gypsies have decayed, and Mr H.E.J. Gibbins in his little book has to retell the old sad story of the misery which results when an unsuitable form of civilisation is thrust upon natures unfitted to receive it. Their numbers are not one-fourth part of what they were ten or twelve years ago, and their racial purity is lost. The tent-dwelling Stanleys and Lees have vanished, and the most common 'Gypsy' surnames are now Barnes, Blake, Cooper, Doe, Green, Lakey, Miles, Pateman, Pearce, Peters, Rose, Sherrard, Sherred, Sherwin, Sherwood, Stone, Wareham, Wells and White, to which might be added James and Penfold.

Even the language of the Romany has quite died out; according to Mr Gibbins, 'it is absolutely unknown to any of them now'; and, 'they do not appear to pick up any folk-lore or legends of other parts or people they meet with worthy of remark.' But we think he is mistaken, and that these statements indicate nothing more than that the author has failed to win the complete confidence of his Gypsies.

Very harmless are the 'New Forest Royalty'. They are abjectly poor, yet vice and immorality are as far from their camps as is religion. 'Emotional but not intellectual' – such is Mr Gibbins' description – amenable to kindness, affectionate, 'civil and polite, most inoffensive, and never known to commit crimes of robbery or violence' - 'A little poaching in the Forest and pilfering are their worst offences.'

One Gypsy characteristic they have retained – the one of all others which, under the circumstances, they could best do without. 'Privations, afflictions, discomfort, and extreme poverty, wet, cold or hunger, sickness and distress, all seem as nothing to them ; but FREEDOM, absolute freedom, with semi-starvation, is EVERYTHING.' And so they refuse regular work on the farms, desert the cottages in which philanthropists have placed them, spurn the offers of the emigration agent, and cling blindly to a forest which no longer affords the means of subsistence nor even a market for their clothes-pegs and fortune-telling.

And if we doubt whether Mr Gibbins' cure – compulsory house-dwelling – is likely to prove efficacious to mend the ills of people whose restless instincts have survived every other racial trait, we can at least thank him for a picture of Gypsy decadence drawn with some sympathetic insight into Gypsy character, and with much humour and common-sense. As proof whereof we quote in conclusion the following anecdote: 'Colonel ------, whose name was well known in the Forest years ago, was very strong in his ideas of orthodox marriages with these nomads, and to further his views in this direction would gladly give a gold wedding ring to any Gypsy girl he thought was shortly to be spliced, and many were the tricks played upon his incredulity. Several girls had two rings each, and one - more artful, perhaps, than the rest – made her boast that she had secured three from him, and yet was not married, nor likely to be.'"

In the same year that Gibbins' book was published, William Pateman was baptised on 11 July 1909 at Swanwick. This took place during the strawberry and fruit picking season (June/July) at Sarisbury and Swanwick. His parents were Mary Jane and Ralph John Pateman, a traveller from Ham.

Emily Pateman married Eli Gregory on 28 March 1910. Emily was the daughter of Thomas and Matilda Pateman. The occupation of the fathers of the bride and groom was given as "Hawker". Emily's sister, Ethel, was a witness.

James Pateman (son of Ralph John and Mary Jane) was baptised on 19 November 1911 and his sister, Alice Lilian, was baptised on 19 July 1914.

Frank Cuttriss
Frank Cuttriss was a photographer from Lyndhurst whose real name was F.R.Hinkins. In 1915 Frank Cuttriss wrote *Romany Life*, a Mills and Boon classic which contains a very good account of "Romany Life experienced and observed during many years of friendly intercourse with the Gypsies. Illustrated with a large number of unique photographs, and other pictures by the author."

The illustrations include "articles of daily life, Gypsy tent, jewellery, styles of hair dressing, method of carrying baby and basket, around the camp fire, types of living-wagon, the maker of toy chairs, camp of clothes-peg makers, bunching 'daffies' and the true 'patcran' :

"The true patrin or pateran usually consists of leaves or grass thrown down in a certain manner by the wayside to guide Gypsies in following the main party, which may have gone forward several days. As the arrangement differs with different families, and a variation in the arrangement may affect its signification, a non-Gypsy is not likely to gain much information should he chance to discover a pateran. In the event of it being necessary to cross a city or town, modifications of the patrin are used, so that notwithstanding the turns taken in passing from one side of the place to the other, the straggler is enabled to find the exact route taken and follow unerringly. If several families from different localities were to pass through a city at about the same time, using the same roadways for a part or the whole of the way, a Gypsy could tell how many families had passed through a certain street and the direction they took, and would identify his own family sign."

A review of *Romany Life* was published in the *Journal of the Gypsy Lore Society* in 1915:

"Romany life as lived by the average Gypsy is certainly rather a haphazard, ill-arranged, and rambling affair: but that is hardly a reason why a book on it should share the same characteristics; and I fear it cannot be denied that Mr Cuttriss's work does share them. The author evidently has a considerable acquaintance with the travellers who haunt the New Forest and that neighbourhood, and has made a conscientious endeavour to describe their mode of life and his experiences among them. But a rambling style and the introduction of rather pointless conversations have prevented him from conveying a very clear impression of either.

Apart from the illustrations, the best part of the book is the minute description of petty details of camp construction and equipment, the manufacture of small articles for hawking, and feminine fashions, many of them illustrated by diagrams and drawings. It is no doubt well to have had these things described by one who is an accurate observer, so far as this experience goes; but whether they were worth the trouble taken is rather doubtful. The earrings and fashions of hair-dressing described and illustrated are only Gypsy in so far as they are antiquated among *gaje*, except for one or two which are obviously eccentric among either. Personally I have not noticed the preference Mr Cuttriss seems to find for cowrie-shaped beads, nor do his photographs support his theory very well; and he is probably influenced by the desire he shows at times to look towards India and the ends of the earth for parallels, when it would be more to the point to look in the nearest pawn-shop window, whence, as he admits elsewhere, the Gypsy trinkets probably came at one time or another.

The trades he mentions are mostly those practiced by the lowest class of *posrat* or *gajo* travellers in the South of England and can hardly rank as Gypsy trades at all. The tent he describes and illustrates is the wagon-tilt type common in the south of England and the Midlands: but he makes no mention of the bee-hive type or the large oval tents of East Anglia and the North of England. More local still is the type of fireplace he illustrates - a fire built on a flat tray – the normal thing in most parts of England being a much pierced bucket raised off the ground by bricks. Some ten years ago an attempt was made in the Midlands, at any rate, to replace it by a large fish-saucepan, not pierced, but with the bottom knocked out: but the fashion soon went out, as it did not draw as well as the pierced bucket. Peculiar to the extreme South of England too are the tripods and the horizontal pole resting on two upright sticks as supports for the kettle, the bent crowbar type of kettle-prop, also illustrated, being universal elsewhere.

The elaborate developments of the simple *patteran*, indicating the composition of the party, who have gone on, by long and short sticks for men and women, a piece of heather with many branches for children, and a bent stick further on if they were on foot, or a straight one if they had a van, will be quite new to most readers. Though elaborate *patterans* are found among foreign Gypsies, they do not assume this form, and Mr Cuttriss is no doubt right in inferring that it is a recent local development.

Careful and accurate as he is in describing things that he can see and feel, and independent in his observations, it is a pity that he should lose these characteristics when treating of other matters. His list of Gypsy surnames shows an unfortunate propensity for following in old tracks, and a lack of judgement in departing from them. Bosswel, Boswell and Bosvil, occur as three different names, simply because previous writers have spelled the name in different ways. The inevitable Corrie turns up again, and so does Glover, for which I know no evidence except Hoyland's list and those which are copied from it; and if ever there was such a family, it is probably extinct long ago.

Though the Wood, Heron or Hearn, Lock and Gray clans are not thought worthy of mention, names like Willett, Black, Harris, Lakey, Sherred, and Rickman appear among the 'principal Romany families'. Yet the people who bear them have an infinitesimally small quantity of Gypsy blood in their veins, if any at all. Again, it is difficult to see how the Fenners can possibly be regarded as one of the principal Gypsy families, though there is good Gypsy blood in the few who exist. The clan originated in the marriage of Joe Fenner, a Buckinghamshire gamekeeper, with Penheli (Penelope) daughter of Timothy ("Doctor") Buckland and Mary Hearn, about ninety years ago. They had the usual baker's dozen or more of children, but only four boys and three girls lived to grow up. The daughters all married young and so changed their name: of the sons the eldest, Hector, was transported for horse-stealing while still a youth; two others had no children, so far as I have been able to discover, and both are dead. The other son, Cornelius, had two families by different wives, but the first passes under the mother's name – Smith – and is settled, while the second contained but one son – as yet unmarried - to carry on the name, beside several daughters, who all married, and all but one of whom are dead. There can therefore never have been more than twenty Gypsies including children alive at the same time bearing the name Fenner, and that hardly constitutes one of the 'principal families'.

Even more misleading, unless I am mistaken, is the insertion of the name Churen on that list. It is a most un-English looking name, and I have never met it as a Gypsy or as a *gajo* name: so I cannot help thinking that Mr Cuttriss copied it from some newspaper, which misprinted the name Choron borne by the foreign Gypsy Coppersmiths who visited England some years ago. But, if so, it is quite unwarrantable to include it in a list of English Gypsy names. Equally unwarrantable is the adoption of the form *aok* for *yok* – derived ultimately from Grellmann – in a list of words, which might be supposed to be English Romani. *Prala* too occurs in this foreign form and is attributed to an English Gypsy woman sufficiently ignorant of her language to say *tacho Romadi* and *cosh*. One may be perfectly certain that it would not occur if it did not appear in Borrow's *Lavo-Lil* and there is a suspiciously strong Borrovian flavour about all the Romani used in the book. Weird compounds like *drom sikkering engr boronashemescrutan*, odd forms like *pawnugo* and *dado*, rare words like *praio* and *tippoty* – which is not a Romani word at all, but an English dialect word – occur throughout, and one would feel more certain about them, if they differed sometimes a little from the form used by Borrow. If Mr Cuttriss had been as careful in listening, as he was in observing, probably he would have found that many of these words occurred in the Romani that he talked to the Gypsies and not in their answers.

His excursions into philology are even more unfortunate. He would derive the name Dosha from *dusta* or *dush*, when it is nothing but a shortened form of Theodosia. He rakes up an obscure Spanish form *minrio* for the ordinary foreign Gypsy *minor*, apparently to account for the final *i* in *mini* – which rather surprisingly, considering how common it is in the South of England, he seems to have heard only once – though that final *i* obviously is nothing but the feminine ending used as an indeclinable form, as it frequently is in modern broken Romani. It is equally necessary to go to Spain to account for the simple intrusion of a vowel between two consonants in *matchiko*. It would have been much more to the point, if he had noted that this is no new form in the New Forest district, as it was recorded from a Hampshire Lee a hundred years ago by Irvine, who spelled it *machuku* and *machuker*. Among the Whites, Coopers, Patemans and other Gypsies, who are generally round Bournemouth, the form used is *macikel*: and I am rather surprised to find no instance of this –*el* ending, which is attached by these Hampshire Gypsies to other words too, for instance *vasabel, verdel*, in this book, unless it is the very corrupt *chuvvel* for *coka*, which occurs in the worst version yet recorded of one of the few English Gypsy songs.

The photographs which illustrate the book are excellent, though occasionally better Gypsy types might have been selected"

The Great War
Cuttriss's book was published during the Great War, which affected most communities, including Thorney Hill. One side effect of the war was a number of marriages – when men left for the front it was by no means certain that they would return home, and this lead couples to tie the knot, just in case the worse happened:

Ethel Pateman married William Feltham on 1 February 1916. William was a soldier from Springbourne, near Bournemouth. Ethel was the daughter of Tom and Matilda Pateman. Emily's sister, Mary, was a witness.

Priscilla Pateman married Charles Turner on 28 December 1916. Charles was a soldier from Christchurch. Priscilla was another daughter of Tom and Matilda Pateman. Priscilla's sisters, Ethel and Alice, were witnesses.

Frederick Pateman (son of Ralph John and Mary Jane) was baptised on 24 September 1916.

Other signs on the pateran trail are to be found on the war memorial which stands guard over the churchyard at All Saints Church, Thorney Hill. Designed by Sir Herbert Baker, this memorial records the names of 18 local men from Thorney Hill who gave their lives for King and Country, including Walter and Harry Pateman.

Walter Pateman was born and lived in Thorney Hill. He enlisted at Winchester as Private 22494 in the 1st Battalion of the Hampshire Regiment. He served in France and Flanders and was killed in action on Friday 1 September 1916. He was buried in the Railway Dugouts Burial Ground, Zillebeke, Ieper, West-Vlaanderen, Belgium, in grave VI.L.20.

Walter was the son of Thomas and Matilda Pateman of Thorney Hill. Thomas is buried at All Saints Thorney Hill and his gravestone reads "Thomas Pateman, 27 April 1929, age 69; son Walter (Tom) Pateman, who fell in action in France 1 September 1916, age 26".

A news item about Private W.T. Pateman appeared in the *Christchurch Times* on 1 September 1917: "Mr and Mrs Thomas Pateman, of Thorney Hill, whose son was killed last year, have received the following letter from the Officer of his Platoon:

'Pte. Pateman, who was killed during our last turn in the trenches, was in my Platoon, and I am writing to express my deepest sympathy with you, and to tell you the circumstances in which he met his death. He was working in the trenches at night, and was hit in the neck by a bullet. He was killed instantly and suffered no pain. He was buried the next night by the Chaplain of the Battalion. He died, as so many fine men have died out here, doing his duty. Not in the excitement of an attack but merely carrying on, he had the bad luck to be hit. Out here we knew him as a sound soldier, and a cheerful man under all circumstances. All who knew him will, I am sure, sympathise sincerely with you in your loss. I remain, Yours truly, C.J.GIRLING, 2nd Lieut., O.C.15th Platoon, 1st Hampshire Regt.'

Harry Pateman was born in Christchurch and lived in Fleet. He enlisted at Winchester as Private 23221, in the Hampshire Regiment. He later became Private 22231, in the 1st Battalion of the Dorsetshire Regiment. He served in France and Flanders and was killed in action on Tuesday 3 July 1917, age 35. He was buried in the Nieuwpoort Communal Cemetery, Nieuwpoort, West-Vlaanderen, Belgium, in grave l.B.2. Harry was the son of John and Rowena Pateman, of 15, Red Lion Row, Windsor.

Another Pateman who fell in the Great War was Major Wilfred Pateman, a Private in the 21st Battalion of the Bedfordshire Regiment, who died aged 23 on Friday 23 August 1918. He is buried at the Achiet le Grand Communal Cemetery Extension, Pas de Calais, France. He was the son of Major and Mary Jane Pateman of Luton Road, Toddington, Bedfordshire.

As was noted earlier, the distinctive name of Major appears in the New Forest Pateman family. William, the first child of Jane and John Pateman (a travelling basket maker from Toddington, Bedfordshire) was born at Bisham on the Berkshire / Buckinghamshire border in 1830. John and Jane may have had at least two more sons – Major and Sidney Pateman. A direct line of travel can be drawn from Toddington and Bisham to Woodmancote and Beaulieu in the New Forest. It is possible that Major and Mary Jane Pateman of Toddington, Bedfordshire, may have been related to Jane and John Pateman.

The War Memorial at All Saints, Thorney Hill, also contains the names of 9 men who died during the Second World War, including William Pateman and Joseph Doe. William Pateman was Corporal 1868170, in the 58 Chemical Warfare Coy., Royal Engineers. He died on Tuesday 23 November 1943, age 34. He was buried in the Imphal War Cemetery, India, in grave 9.A.5. William was the son of Ralph John and

Mary Jane Pateman, of Thorney Hill, and the husband of Lavinia Alice Pateman, of Thorney Hill. They had one child, Roy, born 1937.

Joseph Doe died on Thursday 3 December 1942, age 34. Joseph was a Private 5494813 in the second Battalion of the Hampshire Regiment. He is buried in grave I.D.11 at the Massicault War Cemetery in Tunisia. Joseph was the son of Alfred and Nora Doe and the husband of Emily Doe of Thorney Hill. As was stated earlier, there were many connections between the Pateman and Doe families.

When Eve Draws Nigh Home Lights Appear
When Eve Draws Nigh Home Lights Appear is one of my favourite paintings by Amelia Goddard. It depicts a brightly painted Gypsy vardo and a bender tent. It is getting dark and the horses are resting. There is a group of Gypsies in front of the vardo, gathered around the yog. A woman is approaching the encampment carrying a lantern and she is surrounded by a circle of light. Whether she is one of the family or a visitor, you know that she is about to receive a warm welcome.

Brian Vesey-Fitzgerald received a warm welcome from the Gypsies he got to know. In his book *Gypsies of Britain – an introduction to their history* he talks about the Gypsy families who he met while he was at public school "where on Sundays we were allowed to go for walks by ourselves if we wished to do so. I got then to know several families who visited the area – Lees, Coopers, Stanleys, Scamps, Deightons, Drapers, Patemans, and can remember the names well."

Later he got to know one of the New Forest Gypsies, Amos Churen, really well. It is from Amos that he learnt most about the history and culture of Gypsies. In his chapter on Marriage he relates the following story:

"Amos Churen had seen the thrashing of an erring wife when he was a young man, and told me that one of the Patemans had shaved his wife's head and forced her to wear no covering either to her head or body for two days when, on his return from Germany where he had been a prisoner for three years, he found that she had been unfaithful."

In his section on burials he describes the burial of Caroline Penfold, who was only twenty-six when she died from tuberculosis on 15 April 1926: "The funeral was attended by Gypsies from a wide area, and also by many *poshrats*. Among the names of those that attended were Roberts, Pinfold, Gray, Birch, Holland, Stanley, Lee, Smith, Penfold, Manley, Pateman and Darling."

In his chapter on Gypsies today he explains "the *patteran*, properly the *patrin*. The *patrin* is, of course, the sign left on the road by Gypsies to indicate which way they have taken. It may be a few leaves, or a stick or two, or a handful of grass, but is arranged in such a way as to leave a perfectly clear message for those that follow after. The most common form is a cross with the long arm pointing the way taken.

The *patrin* is common to Gypsies all over the world, but has naturally undergone certain local or national developments. In England to-day it is not much used except among south country Gypsies, and particularly those of Hampshire and the New Forest. Here, development at one time attained an extraordinary degree, and though this has not been maintained at the full it is still very much more complex than anywhere else in Britain. Here, for example, bent sticks are used to indicate travellers on foot, straight sticks to indicate travellers with vans. These sticks are placed a little way from the directional signs. Then branched twigs, or a sprig of heather, or a spray of gorse is laid down to indicate a family with children, and so on. The Gypsy coming upon these signs will know more or less when they were put down and knowing roughly how fast people travel will know pretty well how far ahead his friends are and where he is likely to meet them.

At the same time the patrin of these New Forest and Hampshire Gypsies varies very much from family to family, so that some of the information contained in the signs is possible of interpretation only by members of the family. All the same, the various family *patrins* do get fairly well known. When with Amos Churen I have more than once come across *patrins* by the wayside, and he has stopped and examined them and then said: 'Dey is Patemans', or Lees or Barneys or Stanleys as the case may be."

6. Chronology

Births
7 December 1860, Harriett Pateman, Major & Louisa (Doe), basket maker, Wootton, Milton
1870, June, William Pateman, Christchurch
1877, June, Mary Jane Pateman, Christchurch
1879, March, Caroline Pateman, Christchurch
1879, March, Walter George Pateman, Christchurch
1880, June, Alfred Pateman, Christchurch
1880, June, Lilian Annie, Christchurch
1881, March, Willie Pateman, Christchurch
1882, March, Mary Jane Pateman, New Forest
1882, June, Harry Pateman, Christchurch
1882, June, William George, Christchurch
1884, June, Ellen Pateman, Christchurch
1884, June, George Pateman, Christchurch
1884, September, Emma Rose Pateman, Christchurch
1886, March, Alice Louisa Pateman, Christchurch
1886, June, George Pateman, Christchurch
1886, June, Sidney Charles Pateman, Christchurch
1886, June, (Female) Pateman, Christchurch
1887, June, Frederick Pateman, Christchurch
1888, March, Emily Pateman, Christchurch
1889, September, Frank Pateman, Christchurch
1890, March, Walter Pateman, Christchurch
1890, September, Tom Harris Pateman, Chrustchurch
1892, March, Ethel Pateman, Christchurch
1893, March, (Female) Pateman, Christchurch
1893, September, Emily Gwendoline Pateman, Wimborne
1894, March, Priscilla Pateman, Christchurch
1895, March, Dorothy Pateman, Wimborne
1901, December, John Pateman, Christchurch
1903, June, Job Pateman, Christchurch
1905, March, George Pateman, Christchurch
1907, March, Rosie Gladys, Christchurch
1909, March, Charles John Pateman, Lymington
1909, June, Willie Pateman, Christchurch

Baptisms
10 March 1813, Mary Pateman (?), William and Jane, Christchurch
23 October 1814, Eliza Pateman (?), William & Elizabeth, labourer, Christchurch
25 June 1820 (born 4 June 1820), Elizabeth Jane Major, William and Mary, labourer Christchurch
3 March 1823 (born 12 January 1823), Frances Pitman, John & Elizabeth, labourer, Christchurch
2 April 1825 (born 1 December 1824), Elizabeth Pitman, John & Elizabeth, Waterditch
10 June 1832, Charles Pateman, John & Jane, travelling basket maker, Ham Woodmancote

24 May 1833 (born 11 April 1833), Lydia Pitman, Isaac & Charlotte, labourer, Burton
24 August 1834 (born 27 June 1834), George Pittman, Isaac & Charlotte, labourer, Burton
? September 1835 (born 25 July 1835), Emma Pittman, Isaac & Charlotte, Burton
4 March 1838 (born 6 January 1838), Selina Pittman, Isaac & Charlotte, Burton
20 August 1854, Olive* Pateman, William & Mary Ann, Holyb'ne, lab'r, New Forest (* Oleph crossed out), Ham Holybourne
20 August 1854, Matilda Pateman, William & Mary Ann, Holybourne, labourer, New Forest, Ham Holybourne
15 May 1856, John Bateman, William & Mary Ann, Minstead, HAM, basket maker
28 September 1862, Harriett Pateman, Major & Louisa, Lymington, basket maker, Ham Binsted
13 September 1863, Olive Pateman, Major & Louisa, Lymington, basket maker, Ham Binsted
13 September 1863, Mary Jane Pateman, William & Mary Anne, Christchurch, Hants, basket maker, Ham Binsted
16 September 1866, Sidney Pateman, Sidney & Louisa, Lymington, basket maker, Ham Binsted
08 September 1868, Peter Pateman, Sidney & Louisa, Christchurch, basket maker, Ham Binsted
19 November 1877 (born 11 May 1877), Mary Jane Pateman, William & Elizabeth, Thorney Hill
22 September 1878, Pati(ence?) Pateman, Job & Louisa, Christchurch, labourer, Ham Binsted
11 November 1878 (born 7 January 1878) Ralph John Corbin, John Pateman & Rowena Corbin, Thorney Hill
16 February 1879 (born 14 January 1879) Caroline Pateman, William & Elizabeth, Thorney Hill
16 February 1879 (born 14 January 1879) Walter George Pateman, John & Rowena, Thorney Hill
14 September 1884, Ellen Mary Pateman, Thomas & Mathilda, Binsted, hawker, Ham Binsted
14 September 1884, Caroline Pateman, Thomas & Mathilda, Binsted, hawker, Ham Binsted
05 September 1886, Alice Louisa Pateman, Thomas & Matilda, Christchurch (Twynham), Ham Selborne
25 October 1886, George Pateman, Job & Louisa, Kinson, hawker, Dor Kinson
18 June 1888, Emily Pateman, Thomas & Matilda, Thorney Hill, basket maker, Ham Burley
11 May 1891, Ethel Pateman, Thomas & Matilda, Gipsey labourer, Thorney Hill
16 February 1897 (born 25 June 1889) Frank Pateman, William & Elizabeth, Thorney Hill
13 March 1901, George Pateman, William & Elizabeth, labourer, Thorney Hill
30 March 1902 (born 1 September 1901) John Pateman, John & Mary, Thorney Hill
26 February 1905 (born 2 January 1905), George Henry Pateman, John & Mary, labourer, Thorney Hill
28 July 1907, Sidney Pateman, Sidney & Mary Anne, Locks Heath, traveller, Ham Sarisbury

04 April 1909, Charles Henry Pateman, Sydney & Mary Anne, Park Gate, Sarisbury, labourer, Ham Sarisbury

11 July 1909, William Pateman, John & Mary, Swanwick, traveller, Ham Sarisbury

Marriages
1877, March, William Pateman, Christchurch
1878, December, John Pateman, Christchurch
1887, March, Job Pateman, Christchurch
1902, December, Mary Pateman, Christchurch (27 October 1902)
1904, September, Mary Jane Pateman, Christchurch (10 September 1904)
1905, January, Alice Pateman, Christchurch (24 April 1905)
1907, December, Charles Henry Pateman, New Forest
1910, March, Emily Pateman, Christchurch (28 March 1910)
1911, December, Emma Pateman, Southampton
1912, September, Tom Pateman, Cooper, Christchurch
1916, March, Ethel Pateman, Feltham, Christchurch (1 February 1916)
1916, June, Lillie Pateman, Scott, Christchurch
1916, December, Priscilla Pateman, Turner, Christchurch (28 December 1916)
1923, June, John Pateman, White, Christchurch (2 April 1923)
1924, September, Dorothy Pateman, Ward, Christchurch
1926, September, Edna Pateman, Sale, Bournemouth

Church Weddings
22 July 1834, Naomi Bateman / Peatman (born 1809) married William Doe at Lasham
21 January 1901, John Pateman, 23, labourer, Wallisdown, John, labourer; Mary Pateman, 19 years, Wallisdowne, Job, labourer
27 October 1902, Mary Pateman, 18, spinster, Thorney Hill, Thomas, labourer; John Jeff, 22, bachelor, labourer, Thorney Hill, Walter, labourer ; Noah Burton & Alice Pateman
10 September 1904, Mary Jane Pateman, 27, spinster, Thorney Hill, William, brickmaker; Bertie Broomfield, 27, batchelor, brick maker, Thorney Hill, Albert, brick maker; Beatrice Broomfield, George & Caroline Pateman
24 April 1905, Alice Pateman, 20, spinster, Thorney Hill, Thomas, labourer; Frederick White, 21, bachelor, labourer, Thorney Hill, Richard, labourer; Emily Pateman & John Jeff
28 March 1910, Emily Pateman, 22, spinster, Thorney Hill, Tom, hawker; Eli Gregory, 23, bachelor, labourer, Thorney Hill, Alfred, hawker; Ethel Pateman
1 February 1916, Ethel Pateman, 24, spinster, Thorney Hill, Tom, labourer ; William Feltham, 23, bachelor, soldier, 56 Capstone Road, Springbourne, William, cab driver; Fred White & Mary Jeff
28 December 1916, Priscilla Pateman, 23, spinster, Bransgore, Tom, market gardener; Charles Turner, 24, bachelor, soldier, Christchurch, Mark, coast guard; Ethel Feltham & Alice White
2 April 1923, John Pateman, 21, bachelor, labourer, Thorney Hill, Joseph, labourer; Sarah White, 20, spinster, Thorney Hill, Leonard, labourer; Rose & George Pateman

Deaths
1858, March, Jane Pateman, Lymington
1864, March, George Pateman, Christchurch (27 February 1864)
1867, December, Charles Pateman, 35, New Forest
1873, December, Thomas Pateman, 85, Christchurch
1881, March, Willie Pateman, 0, Christchurch (9 April 1881)
1886, June, Female, 0 Christchurch
1887, March, John Pateman, 30, Christchurch (28 March 1887)
1892, March, William Pateman, 55, Christchurch (19 February 1892)
1893, March, Female, 0, Christchurch (13 March 1893)
1909, March, Mary Pateman, 72, Christchurch (7 April 1909)
1909, June, Mary Pateman, 72, Christchurch
1918, September, Alfred Pateman, 38, Christchurch (2 October 1918)
1922, June, Elizabeth Pateman, 67, Christchurch (24 April 1922)
1923, September, Job Pateman, 20, Christchurch (16 July 1923)
1929, June, Thomas Pateman, 69, Bournemouth (30 April 1929)
1937, September, William Pateman, 94, Christchurch (14 September 1937)
1938, March, Louisa Pateman, 76, Christchurch
1938, September, Job Pateman, 79, Bournemouth
1940, March, Charles Pateman, 78, Bournemouth
1942, June, Walter Pateman, 64, Southampton
1944, September, Annie Pateman, 68, Southampton
1945, March, Ralph Pateman, 67, Christchurch (1 February 1945)
1945, September, Emily Pateman, 76, Bournemouth
1955, September, Eliza Pateman, 62, Christchurch
1957, December, Ray Pateman, 20, Christchurch (24 October 1957)
1958, December, Mary Pateman, 78, Christchurch
1959, December, Matilda Pateman, 94, Christchurch

Burials
27 February 1864, George Pateman, Thorney Hill, 14 years
1 March 1881, John Pateman, Thorney Hill, 1 month
9 April 1886, William Pateman, Thorney Hill, 13 days, not baptised
28 March 1887, John Pateman, Thorney Hill, 30 years
12 February 1892, William Pateman, Thorney Hill, 55 years
13 March 1893, Infant daughter of Rose Pateman, Thorney Hill, 13 days
7 April 1909, Mary Pateman, Union Work House, Christchurch, 72 years
2 October 1918, Alfred Pateman, Thorney Hill, 38 years, All Saints
24 April 1922, Elizabeth Pateman, Thorney Hill, 67 years, All Saints
16 July 1923, Job Pateman, Thorney Hill, 20 years, All Saints
30 April 1929 (died 27 April 1929), Thomas Pateman, Forest Side, Thorney Hill, 69 years, All Saints
14 September 1937, William Pateman, Thorney Hill, 94 years, All Saints
1 February 1945 (died 29 January 1945), Ralph John Pateman, 8 Council Houses, Thorney Hill, 67 years, All Saints
24 October 1957 (died 20 October 1957), Roy W Pateman, 20 years, All Saints
? 1958 Mary Jane Pateman, 76 years, All Saints
? 1965, George Henry Pateman, 60 years, All Saints

7. Families

William Pateman and Jane?
Mary (1813)

William Pateman and Elizabeth?
Eliza (1814)

John Pitman (1784) and Elizabeth? (1785)
Elizabeth (1821)
Frances (1823)
Elizabeth (1826)
Thomas (1828)

John Pateman and Jane?
Peggy [aka Margaret Curtis] (1828) = Francis Doe
William (1830-1892)
Charles (1832-1867)
Major = Louisa Doe
Sidney = Louisa?

Isaac Pitman (1810) and Charlotte? (1811)
Lydia (1833)
George (1834)
Emma (1835)
Susanah (1837)
Selina (1838)
Anna Maria (1841)
Isabella (1843)
Albert (1845)
Keith (1848)

William Pateman (1830-92) and Mary Ann James (1833-1909)
William (1848-1937) = Elizabeth (1855-1922)
George (1850-1864)
Olive/Nell (1852)
Mary Ann (1853)
Matilda (1854) = Henry Osborne
John (1856-1887) = Rowena Corbin (1860)
Job (1859-1938) = Louisa Ayre (1862-1938)
Thomas (1860-1929) = Matilda (1865-1959)
Mary Jane (1863)
John (1878)

Major Pateman and Louisa Doe
Harriett (1862)
Olive (1863)

Sidney Pateman and Louisa?
Sidney (1866)
Peter (1868)

William Pateman (1848-1937) and Elizabeth Harris (1855-1922)
Charles (1874) step son
Mary Jane (1877) = Bertie Broomfield (1877)
Caroline (1879)
Alfred (1880-1918)
William (1883)
George (1884)
Frederick (1887)
Frank (1889)
George (1901)

Matilda Pateman (1854) and Henry Osborne
Harry (1877)
William (1882)
George (1885)
Lilian (1889) = ?Scott
Charles (1892)
Albert (1896)

Job Pateman (1859-1938) and Louisa Ayre (1862-1938)
Patience (1878-1960) = Henry Doe (1874-1943)
Edith (1880)
Mary Jane (1882-1958)
Agnes (1884)
George (1886)
William (1888)
Job (1890)
Dorothy (1897)
Alice Amelia (1905)

John Pateman (1856-1887) and Rowena Corbin (1860)
Ralph John (1878-1945) = Mary Jane Pateman (1882-1958)
Walter George (1879-1942)
Lilian Ellen (1880)
Harry (1882-1917)
Rose (1885)
Sidney (1886) = Mary Ann = Phyliss
Tom (1891) = ?Cooper

Thomas Pateman (1860-1929) and Matilda (1865-1959)
Caroline (1884)
Ellen Mary (1884) = John Jeff (1880)
Alice Louisa (1886) = Frederick White (1884)
Emily (1888) = Eli Gregory (1887)
Walter Thomas (1890-1916)
Ethel (1891) = William Feltham (1893)
Priscilla (1893) = Charles Turner (1892)

Patience Pateman (1878-1960) and Henry Doe (1874-1943)
Alice (1897) = William Doe (1898)
Patience (1898) = John Henry Cooper (1898)
Henry (1900-1976) = Selina Cooper (1902-1978)
Britannia (1906) = Nelson Stokes
Nelson (1910) = Milly Rickman
Job (1914) = Rosie Saxby
William = Janey Keets
Louisa = George Jones
John = Mary Scott

Edith Pateman (1880) and William Doe (1851)
Willie (1898)
Job (1900-1923)
Rosie (1901)

Ralph John Pateman (1878-1945) and Mary Pateman (1882-1958)
John (1901-1977) = Sarah White (1902-1987)
George Henry (1905-1965)
Rose (1907) = Leonard White (1905)
William (1909-1943) = Alice Baker (1914-1984)
James (1911)
Alice Lilian (1914-1984) = Percy Kennell (1906)
Frederick (1916-1974) = Doris Graves
Harry Sidney (1919)
Ronald (1922-1996)
John James (1923-1996)
Mary (1925)

Sidney Pateman and Mary Anne?
Sidney (1907)
Charles Henry (1909)
Mary Ann (1915)
Rose (1917)

?Pateman and ?Pateman
Jim (1911)

?Pateman and ?Hughes
Thomas (1920)

Census

<u>1851</u>

Burley / Christchurch
William Pitman, 38, brick layer, Hursley
Mary Ann Pitman, 36, ?
Henry Pitman, 6, scholar, Hursley
George Pitman, 4, Hursley
Mary Jane Pitman, 2, Hursley

Isaac Pitman, 41, gardener, Hursley
Charlotte Pitman, 40, Winkton
Sussanah Pitman, 14, Hursley
Selina Pitman, 13, Hursley
Anna Maria Pitman, 10, Hursley
Isabella Pitman, 8, Hursley
Albert Pitman, 6, Hursley
Keith Pitman, 3, Hursley

John Pitman, 67, ag lab, Burley
Elizabeth Pitman, 66, Burley
Eliza Pitman, 30, Burley
Elizabeth Pitman, 25, Burley
Thomas Pitman, 23, Burley

Emma Pitman, 15, house servant, Hursley

Lydia Pitman, 84, Burley

<u>1861</u>

Thorney Hill, Bransgore
William Peatman, 32, labourer, Christchurch
Mary Ann Peatman, 28, Christchurch
William Peatman, 13, labourer, Christchurch
George Peatman, 11, Christchurch
Nell Peatman, 9, Christchurch
Matilda Peatman, 7, Christchurch
John Peatman, 5, Christchurch
Job Peatman, 3, Christchurch
Thomas Peatman, 7 months, Christchurch
Francis Dough, lodger, 18, labourer, Lymington

<u>1871</u>

Hill Top, Thorney Hill, Bransgore
William Pateman, 46, labourer, Christchurch
Mary Pateman, 42, Bucks, Bisin
William Pateman, 23, labourer, Burley

John Pateman, 15, Minstead
Job Pateman, 12, Harbridge
Thomas Pateman, 11, Harbridge
George, orphan, 12, Wimborne
Mary A, 18, Beer, Dorset
Jane, 8, Thorney Hill

Denny Lodge near North Gate Rd & King's Hat Inclosure
Nehemias Doe, head, married, 24, basket and clothes peg maker, New Forest
Ruth Doe, wife, married, 22, New Forest
Amelia Doe, daughter, 4, New Forest
Albert Doe, son, 2, New Forest
Mary Ann Doe, daughter, 2m, New Foest
William Doe, head, married, 56, tinman, New Forest
Naomi Doe, wife, married, 52, seller of tin wares, New Forest
Albert Doe, son, unmarried, 20, tinman, New Forest
Olive Doe, daughter, 12, New Forest
Job Pateman, servant, unmarried, 15, helper

<u>1881</u>

Thorney Hill
John Pateman, 23, Thorney Hill
Rowena Pateman, 21, Bransgore
Walter Pateman, 2, Thorney Hill
Ellen Pateman, 1, Thorney Hill

William Pateman, 30, Thorney Hill
Elizabeth Pateman, 26, Bransgore
Charles Harris, 7, Bransgore
Mary J Pateman, 3, Bransgore
Caroline Pateman, 2, Thorney Hill
Alfred Pateman, 11m, Thorney Hill

Matthew Jeff, 65, Marchfield, Gloucester
Elizabeth Jeff, 63, Oxford
Mary A. Jeff, 36, Ringwood
Mary A. Pateman, 17, Christchurch
William Jeff, 9, Christchurch
Maria Jeff, 6, Christchurch
Annie Jeff, 4, Christchurch
George Jeff, 1, Christchurch

William Pateman, 52
Mary Pateman, 48
Thomas Pateman, 20, Thorney Hill
John Pateman, 3, Bransgore
George Eggerton, Maidenhead, Berks

Job Pateman, 22, Thorney Hill
Louisa Pateman, 20, Bournemouth
Patience Pateman, 2, Alton
Edith Pateman, 1, Thorney Hill

1891

Park Downs, Banstead, Surrey
Joseph Pateman, 40, travelling Gypsy, Hants, Basingstoke
Mary Pateman, 37, Hants, Andover
Ada Pateman, 19, Andover
Siberina Pateman, 20, Andover
Shipton Pateman, 1, Andover

Thorney Hill
William Pateman, 40, general labourer, Christchurch
Elizabeth Pateman, 37, Christchurch
Charles Harris, step-son, 17, general labourer, Christchurch
Caroline Pateman, 12, Christchurch
Alfred Pateman, 10, Christchurch
William Pateman, 8, Christchurch
George Pateman, 7, Christchurch
Frederick Pateman, 4, Christchurch
Frank Pateman, 1, Christchurch

Thomas Pateman, 31, general labourer, Thorney Hill
Matilda Pateman, 27, Thorney Hill
Mary Pateman, 7, Thorney Hill
Alice Pateman, 5, Thorney Hill
Emily Pateman, 3, Thorney Hill
Thomas Pateman, 1, Thorney Hill

William Pateman, 60, hawker, Bucks, Bisom
Mary Pateman, 55, Hants, Town N.K.
Annie Crutcher, lodger, widow, 40

Sydney James, 48, general labourer, Dorset, Blandford
Louisa James, 46, Ringwood
Job James, 28, Wilts, Redlynch, blind
Dorcas James, 19, Thorney Hill
George James, 16, labourer, Thorney Hill
John James, 13, Thorney Hill
Harry Pateman, 8, nephew, Thorney Hill
Frank James, 8, Thorney Hill

Rose Pateman, 31, widow, hawking on own account, Bransgore
Walter Pateman, 12, Thorney Hill
Lillian A Pateman, 11, Thorney Hill
Rose Pateman, 6, Thorney Hill
Sydney Pateman, 5, Thorney Hill

Tom Pateman, 7m, Thorney Hill

Tent, Redhill Common, Thorney Hill
Job Pateman, 30, Romsey
Louisa Pateman, 31, Dorset, Red Hill
Patience Pateman, 5, Binstead
Edith Pateman, 5, Thorney Hill
Mary Jane Pateman, 9, Wilts, Bramshaw
Agnes Pateman, 7, Thorney Hill
George Pateman, 3, Thorney Hill
William Pateman, 3, Thorney Hill
Job Pateman, 9m, Surrey, Ripley

Eling, Hampshire
In camp with Charles Sherwood & Nehemiah Doe, Hanger Corner, Nr Marchwood, Hampshire: Mathew and Phoebe Jeff and their 8 children; William and Selina Jeff and their 5 children, including Agnes (7, Thorney Hill) and Nahomri (4, Thorney Hill)

1901

Thorney Hill
William Pateman, 50, general labourer, Lyndhurst
Elizabeth Pateman, 46, Christchurch
Alfred Pateman, 20, general labourer, Christchurch
George Pateman, 17, general labourer, Christchurch
Frederick Pateman, 14, Christchurch
Frank Pateman, 11, Christchurch

Thomas Pateman, 36, hawker, Oxbridge
Matilda Pateman, 35, hawker, Bournemouth
Mary Pateman, 17, Thorney Hill
Alice Pateman, 15, Thorney Hill
Emily Pateman, 13, Thorney Hill
Walter Pateman, 11, Thorney Hill
Ethel Pateman, 9, Thorney Hill
Priscilla Pateman, 7, Thorney Hill

Tent, Thorney Hill
James Scott, 24, general labourer, Thorney Hill
Lillie Scott, 22, hawker, Thorney Hill
Violet Scott, 1, Thorney Hill
John Scott, 2m, Thorney Hill
Harry Pateman, lodger, Thorney Hill

8. Sources

Further reading

A Summary Account of the Proceedings of a Provisional Committee associated at Southampton with a view to the consideration and improvement of the Condition of the Gipsies (1828).

Juliette de Bairacli-Levy (1958) *Wanderers in the New Forest,* Faber

Juanita Berlin (1960), The Gypsies of the New Forest, in *The New Forest,* Galley Press

Sven Berlin, *Dromengro* (2003), Finishing Publications Ltd, PO Box 70, 105 Whitney Drive, Stevenage, Hertfordshire, SG1 4DF, www.svenberlin.com

Sven Berlin (2005) *The Other Man,* Finishing Publications

Sven Berlin (1996) *Virgo in exile,* Finishing Publications

Anne Biffin (2003) Holmsley Airfield Memorial in *Nova Foresta Magazine,* Autumn / Winter 2003/04

John Boorman (2003) *Sven Berlin : Paintings from Shave Green 1953-1970,* St. Barbe Museum & Art Gallery

Juanita Casey (2003) Life with Sven – The Wagon Years, in *Sven Berlin Paintings from Shave Green,* St. Barbe Museum & Art Gallery

Rose C. De Crespigny & Horace Hutchinson (1899) *The New Forest its traditions, inhabitants and customs,* John Murray

Henry Thomas Crofton (1907) *Affairs of Egypt,* Journal of the Gypsy Lore Society

Frank Cuttriss (1915) *Romany Life,* Mills & Boon Limited

Brigadier Arthur Fortescue (2005) *All Saints Church Thorney Hill* (text revised and expanded by Canon Patrick Elkins)

Henry Gibbins (1909) *Gipsies of the New Forest and other Tales* , W. Mate and Sons Ltd

Alice E. Gillington (1908) *The House of the Open Door,* Journal of the Gypsy Lore Society

Betty Gillington (1916) *Gypsies of the heath by the Romany Rawny,* Elkin Mathews & Marrot

Gipsies of the New Forest and other tales by Henry E.J. Gibbins (1909) Journal of the Gypsy Lore Society

Tim Goddard (1998) *A Painter of Gypsies,* Romany Routes, Vol.3 No.6

Elizabeth Godfrey (1912) *The New Forest,* Blackie & Son Limited

Hampshire County Council (2003) *Capital funding for voluntary village halls and community centres*

William Howitt (1844) *The Rural Life of England,* Longman, Brown, Green and Longmans

Ruth Lavender (1986) *The Story of Thorney Hill,* Bournemouth Local Study Publications

Steve Marshall (2003) Gold in the Dust – The Gypsy Paintings of Sven Berlin, in *Sven Berlin : Paintings from Shave Green 1953-1970,* St. Barbe Museum & Art Gallery

David Mayall (1988) *Gypsy Travellers in Nineteenth Century Society*, Cambridge University Press

G. Morley, *Smuggling in Hants and Dorset*

M.W. Penfold (1991) *Thorney Hill – this, that and t'other*

Rambler (2003) Of Bricks and Brickworks in *Nova Foresta Magazine,* Autumn / Winter 2003/04

Romany Life by Frank Cuttriss (1915) Journal of the Gypsy Lore Society

Hyman Segal (2003) Sven Berlin – A Man of Truth, in *Sven Berlin : Paintings from Shave Green 1953-1970,* St. Barbe Museum & Art Gallery

Len Smith (2003) The Lost Citizens of the Nevi Wesh, in *Sven Berlin : Paintings from Shave Green 1953-1970,* St. Barbe Museum & Art Gallery

Len Smith (2004) *Romany Nevi-Wesh: an informal history of the New Forest Gypsies,* Nova Foresta Publishing

Irene Soper (1994) *The Romany Way,* Ex Libris Press

Louisa Stokes (1950) *The Love Story of a Gipsy*, Stockwell

Peter Tate (1979) *The New Forest 900 Years after,* Macdonald and Jane's

The Eccentric Mindblowing Detmar Blow (2004) National Trust Magazine

Mike Turner (1999) *New Forest Voices,* Tempus

Brian Vesey-Fitzgerald (1973) *The Gypsies of Britain – an introduction to their history,* Chapman and Hall

Brian Vesey-Fitzgerald (1966) *Portrait of the New Forest*, Robert Hale

GEC Webb (1960) *Gypsies: the secret people*, Herbert Jenkins

Leslie White (1995) *The Holmsley Story*, S&L Publishers

John Wise (1895) *The New Forest: Its History and its Scenery*, Henry Sotheran & Co

Charlotte Young (1892) *An Old Woman's Outlook in a Hampshire Village*

Resources

British Library
Newspapers
Colindale Avenue
London, NW9 5HE
www.bl.uk/collections/newspapers.html

Has copies of national and local newspapers such as *Christchurch Times, Hampshire Post, Morning Leader* and *Northern Echo*

Family Record Centre
1 Myddleton Street
Islington, EC1R 1UW
www.familyrecords.gov.uk

Has records of births, marriages and deaths and the Census 1841-1901 for all English counties.

Hampshire Genealogical Society
198a Havant Road
Drayton
Portsmouth
Hampshire, PO6 2EH
www.hgs-online.org.uk

Has local records, including the Hampshire Burial Index.

Hampshire Gypsies
http://freepages.genealogy.rootsweb.com/~villages/gypsies.htm

This website contains some historical information about Hampshire Gypsies.

Hampshire Record Office
Sussex Street
Winchester, SO23 8TH
www.hants.gov.uk/record-office/catalog/index.html

Parish records, Census, local history books and photographs. Given that Gypsies have lived in the New Forest for over 500 years it is surprising, perhaps, that the Hampshire Record Office only has a dozen references to Gypsies:

- Marchwood Parish Council minutes, include a Gypsy action committee and Gypsy sub committee minutes, 1789/PX9
- 1757, Burial of Gypsy at Burghclere, 148M82PR3
- 1825, John Smith alias Hughes a Gypsy buried at Itchen Abbas, 23M69/PZ4
- 1828, A summary account of the proceedings of a provisional committee associated at Southampton with a view to the consideration and improvement of the condition of the Gypsies, 355/3/2/3
- 1885, Photo of Gypsy hop pickers at Binstead, 153M85/1/page 15
- Early 20th century, photograph of Gypsy camp at Bramshaw Wood, 11M96/31
- 1908-1910, baptisms at Cheriton, 138M82PR5
- 1920's, Alton and District hop pickers mission reports mentions Gypsies, 85M93
- 1929, Gypsies in Hartley Wintney RDC, 59M76/DDC133
- 1946-53, Gypsies on Rye Common, 59M76/DDC144
- 1971, Correspondence re possible pollution of Blackwater River from site of a Gypsy encampment, 8M96/20
- 1973-77, Gypsies encroaching on Hazley Heath, 69M76/DDC152/153

New Forest Museum and Library
Lyndhurst,
Hampshire, SO43 7NY
www.newforestmuseum.org.uk

Has an exhibition about life through the ages in the New Forest and a reference library.

Passing Through
www.passing-through.co.uk

The aim of this website is to record as many census and parish record details of "travelling" people as possible.

Paultons Romany Museum
Paultons Park
Ower
Romsey
Hampshire, SO51 6AL

Extensive display of Romany wagons and artefacts. Well illustrated and informative guide book *Romany Life and Customs* (1990)

Red House Museum and Garden
Quay Road,
Christchurch
Dorset
www.hants.gov.uk/museum/redhouse/

Chronicles the life of people in the Christchurch area over the years. Includes two Gypsy paintings by Amelia Goddard.

St Barbe Museum & Art Gallery
New Street
Lymington
Hampshire, SO41 9BH
www.stbarbe-museum.org.uk

Chronicles the life of people in the Lymington area over the years.

The Living Album – Hampshire's Gypsy Heritage project
www.hants.gov.uk/rh/gypsy

The Living Album – Hampshire's Gypsy Heritage project, began in January 2006 and includes a learning pack, DVD and touring exhibition. The project aims to help members of Hampshire's wider Gypsy and Traveller community to discover and access relevant museum and archive collections in a creative and informative way. It will also help to raise the profile of Gypsy culture within schools, especially those who have Gypsy children in attendance. The project website provides lots of information relating to the history and contemporary culture of Gypsy children and their families and has opened up the history of Gypsy culture and lifestyle in Hampshire to a worldwide audience.

Other books by John Pateman

Canadian Corner: Orpington and the Great War

Charles Dickens and Travellers

Dipper's Slip: the life and times of Noah Pateman

Hoo, Hops and Hods: the life and times of Robert Pateman

Seven Steps To Glory: Private Pateman Goes To War

Three Years on the Western Front: Gunner Rodbourne Goes to War

Tugmutton Common: the life and times of William Pateman

What Dark History is This: William Pateman and the Gordon Riots

These titles are available from Lulu.com.